GODLY STRONG

GODLY STRONG

LOVE LIKE A MAN

By John Helton

ISBN: 978-1-7350307-2-2

PROLOGUE

Note from John:

When I purchased my home, there were little options when it came to internet service. As I did my research, the only company who had internet in our area with speeds faster than dial-up also had a bundle package. That is what we went with, internet, cable, phone, and security system. This package ran approximately $212 per month. Of course, it required a 2-year contract.

As we neared the end of the contract, and with the mindset of wanting to save some money, I decided to call them before the renewal date. The thought was if I got rid of half of the bundle, my price might not be lowered 50%, but probably around 35% - 40%. So, I called the company and asked the customer service rep: "How much would it be if I got rid of my phone and security system?" His response took me a minute to register.

He said, "That would drop the price down to $207. That price would also require a 2-year contract."

Wait. I reduced my package by half and only save $5 per month.

I then asked, "How much is it if I do not go with the 2-year contract?" This was so I could have a little extra time to figure out if there were any other options, or if maybe a new one would soon be available. I did not want to be locked in another contract.

He said, "Without a 2-year contract, it would run you around $367 per month."

With not much time to decide, I started the research again as I did the two years prior. Lo and behold, a really good company had just installed lines in our neighborhood for all of the same services! I got a price, loved the package on internet along with the speed, and switched from cable to live streaming TV. And with no contracts for either! BINGO!

I then called the original company to cancel my service. At that time, they transferred me to a "cancellation specialist" who practically begged me to stay. He came up with an outstanding offer!

"We can give you that same package with all four of your services for $132." Say what?

I then told him I was not interested. He continued putting on the pressure to get me to stay, but to no avail. My mind was made up. I now have No contracts as well as unlimited internet with no governor to slow the speeds down if I used too much internet, etc.

About a week later, another call came in from that same company.

"I want to extend this special offer to you. You can keep the package you currently have which includes phone, internet, television, and the security system for $69 per month."

With a proud demeanor – almost cocky - he continued, "What do you think of THAT?"

"To be honest," I said, "it ticks me off."

He was as stunned as he was confident.

With a confused demeanor he asked, "Why is that?"

I said in a very respectful tone, "Because you did not appreciate me when I was your customer and held the prices up on me. Now that I am ready to walk out the door, you love me. If you had that same value of me when I was your customer, I still might be one."

In other words, do not wait until I am walking out the door to show your love, appreciation, and how much you value me.

But isn't that how we treat our wives in society today? It is not until the wife heads toward the door before the husband realizes he has not cherished or treated her as he should have all along. How that must break the heart of God when His precious daughter is treated in such a way.

Too many husbands wait to honor their wives until they are walking out the door. Or maybe he knew he was not treating her appropriately but took her for granted thinking she would put up with his egomaniacal attitude regardless of how she was being treated. There is no place in the Kingdom of God for that nonsense!

Let me tell you one final story before we hang up (I did that on purpose), and it is incredibly short.

In April 2017, I woke up on a Monday morning and went to work. I woke up that following Tuesday morning planning my wife's funeral.

Let me encourage you to not wait until the funeral to cherish your wife, wishing you had more time to spend with her. You have that opportunity right now! DO! NOT! BLOW! IT!

Thankfully, I cherished her more than life itself and when the funeral rolled around, I can honestly say I had no regrets.

I have since remarried and love that woman with everything in me.

My passion for her burns like a fire in the desert. I can see her purpose because God showed it to me. I see her value as a daughter of the King. I also cannot seem to spend enough time with her and that quirky personality she has; that gorgeous smile, and to hear that adorable laugh.

Although I am legally blind, I still focus on her just to watch her walk. Yes, I watch her walk! That is because I am invested in my wife.

Too many people take life for granted. God forbid you have to experience anything like I did in April 2017. But even if you were promised many more years, make the most of those years and enjoy your wife. The Bible says to do so!!

May this book challenge you, encourage you, and help you be the Godly Strong husband God has called you to be.

It is time to learn how to LOVE LIKE A MAN so you can love like THE man! !

"Yesterday is history.

Tomorrow's a mystery.

Today is a gift.

That's why they call it, 'THE PRESENT.'"

Blessings!

John Helton

"The Blind Fury"

Table of Contents

INTRODUCTION

As a marriage minister, leader, and teacher as well as being a Master Certified Relationship Coach working with struggling marriages and relationships, jointly or individually, I noticed a disturbing trend as I progressed in the ministry.

Too many men were trying to be "macho strong," making every attempt to exhibit their "masculinity" whether it was strutting around with the authoritative, dictatorial attitude, or blatant selfishness; not really caring how their actions affected their wife, or simply not knowing how to be a husband for lack of knowledge.

While there are many more examples of inappropriate behaviors, the bottom line is this:

If you want to be macho strong, you must be Godly Strong! That is what this devotional challenge is designed to do; to help you recognize that the greatest man of all time, Jesus, should be our example. Not what we have been shown in error, not what we have been shown in Hollywood, or the façade of machoness taught by society of what a "real man" is.

In the book of Job, we see God getting a little confrontational with him:

Job 38:1-3

1 Then the Lord spoke to Job out of the storm. He said:

2 "Who is this that obscures my plans with words without knowledge?

3 Brace yourself like a man; I will question you, and you shall answer me.

Marriage is to bring glory to God. God loves the wife, but also loves the wife through the husband. Not being a Godly Strong husband can obscure that plan, as well as obscure your own personal growth. Double whammy! But when you love your wife as "Christ loved the church," you grow personally and your marriage grows as well. Then, the outside world will also see God's glory. And when God asks you questions about your role as a husband, you better "brace yourself like a man" because "YOU WILL ANSWER!"

It is time for men to become Godly Strong for the wife. And although not an extensive topical study, this devotional challenge will give you knowledge and touch on many different areas to help you grow into what God has called you to be as a "Godly Strong Husband!"

Job 38:3

"Gird up now thy loins like a man;" (KJV)

Yikes! But you can "protect yourself" by being who God called you to be. This is the best option; promise!

A stronger marriage = a stronger family; a stro

nger family = a stronger church; and a stronger church = a stronger community!

Proverbs 18:22

"A man's greatest treasure is his wife. She is a gift from the Lord." (CEV)

Throughout this expanded devotional, for each topic, you will be asked challenge questions and also given a "Godly Strong Challenge." The questions are designed to get you thinking and help you grow in the topic discussed. It is encouraged for you to get a notebook to have plenty of space to write down your answers.

Lastly, sin is defined in the Strong's Greek Lexicon as, "missing the mark." As you are honest with yourself with the challenges, determine whether or not you are "missing the mark" in these areas.

NOTE: Consider asking a friend to join you in this journey for accountability, fellowship, and discussion. It is a fantastic way to grow with a friend, and then bless your wife!

TWO BIBLICAL PRINCIPLES TO KNOW

Before getting into the meat, there are two Biblical principles of which to be aware. They are:

- The Law of first mention
- The Law of order

The Law of First Mention

In most cases, the first time something is mentioned in scripture, we can use that as the baseline for that particular topic throughout the rest of scripture.

The Law of Order

1 Corinthians 14:33

God is not a God of disorder, but of peace; in all the congregations of the Lord's people.

This is how He operates! But too many times, we overlook the simplest of things, and that can cause misunderstandings. Here is an example:

How many times, when going through something a bit difficult, someone will tell you, "Well, just resist the devil and he will flee from you!"

Yes, most of us have heard that over the years. So, what is the problem? The problem is that the Bible does not say that! Say what?! Here is what it says:

James 4:7

Submit yourselves, then, to God. Resist the devil, and he will flee from you.

Huge difference! If you want the devil to flee, you must be submitted to God FIRST!

You will see these two principles as you proceed through this book.

LOGOS AND RHEMA

Word Up!

There are two types of "words" found in scripture for our benefit:

- **LOGOS WORD**

This is the Word of God applied in a more general way. It gives us what we need in principle; in more general terms. Statements like, "do not lie," "do not steal," "do not practice sexual immorality," etc.

- **RHEMA WORD**

This is a word given that is more specific to you or your situation. It can come in ways such as:

- The written Word of God
- God speaking to you directly.
- Someone or something God uses to confirm a specific situation, decision, etc. in your life.,

In whatever way the rhema word comes to you, one thing to remember; the rhema word will always line up with the logos word (Word of God).

In short: The logos word is more general and the rhema word is more specific.

---

1 Thessalonians 5:11

Therefore encourage one another and build each other up, just as in fact you are doing.

That is the general Word of God; the "logos" word.

But while you were reading that scripture you hear, "You really need to go encourage your wife right now because she has had a rough day at work."

That, my friend, is the rhema word! God put it on your heart, after reading that verse, to go encourage your wife because you wanted her to know how much you appreciate all she does.

The Godly Strong Challenge

If you read this on a day that ends in the letter "Y," then:

You have to take your wife on a date within the next seven days. It is your job to plan it, pay for it, arrange it, and treat her like a queen!

If the next seven days are impossible, then your first available day must be date night. No excuses! DO IT!

When you return from your date, you must give her a massage. if she does not like that type of thing, then rub her feet, scratch her back, run a warm/hot bath for her, lotion her up, or something that pampers her. She's going to love you for it!

Do this WITHOUT expecting anything in return! If you get something in return; great! If not, remember, this is 100% about your wife and not YOU!

The Godly Strong Challenge #2

What logos word can you apply to this action, and what could be the rhema word?

Write down how your wife responded to the date and to the post-date activity!

WHAT'S LOVE GOT TO DO WITH IT?

Building the Marriage House

The Bible is a never-ending love story. It starts in Genesis and continues through Revelation. 1 Corinthians 13 is even considered "the love chapter."

The word "love" can be found 479 times in the New American Standard Bible. The problem is one type of love you read about in Matthew might not be equivalent to the other "love" you read in Romans. As you very well know, the English word "love" can have different meanings.

We love our siblings with a different love than we love our spouse.

We love our parents with a different love than we love our best friend.

The problem is that we only have one English word to describe each of those types of love. Not so with the Greek language.

That is because the Greek language – in which the New Testament was written – has over 5,000,000 words while the English language is host to approximately 1,000,000 words.

The word "love" can be said in at least three different ways in Greek, but just one in English. That is why the Bible simply uses the English word "love," although they have different meanings.

Because of that, we will start off with explanations of the Greek words and how they apply. Take note of these as they are vitally important to have in your marriage for it to reach its full potential.

Friendship & Brotherly Love

Greek Word: Philia (fil-ee'-ah)

Definition: Beloved, dear, friendly.

OVERVIEW: Just like any friend we have, our friendship with them is conditional. They bring us joy, laughter, and we just have fun being around them, and that is why they are our friends. We base that friendship on what they can give us and vice-versa.

The Strong's Greek Lexicon describes it like this:

"A friend; someone dearly loved (prized) in a personal, intimate way; a trusted confidant, held dear in a close bond of personal affection."

It also describes it as, "experienced based love."

What kind of "experiences" are you cultivating with your wife? Whatever they are, they should be enhancing your friendship with her! Your wife should be your very best friend!

As we build the marriage house, we now know your wife should be viewed permanently as your:

- Best Friend

Romantic Love

Greek Word: Eros

Definition: Romantic and sexual love

Overview: This Greek word is not found in scripture; however, that type of love is.

Eros is where we get the word, "erotic." This is a romantic and sexual love that is designed by God as a gift for one person — and one person only! Your wife! Of course, sex and romance are a "feeling" and a good one at that! This is why it is a conditional type of love much like **philia**. Not only does it bring happiness, but it also unites you to your wife in the most intimate of ways. Oh, and it is fun!

Building the marriage house:

- Best Friend
- Lover

Unconditional Love

Greek Word: Agapé (ag-ah'-pay)

Definition: Love, goodwill; The type of love God prefers.

OVERVIEW: One simple explanation of this word is so powerful, there is really no reason to elaborate much. Simply keep this in mind when loving your wife.

"Love your wife based on YOUR character; not HERS!"

This is an unconditional, God-like (divine) love.

Basic steps to love Agape style:

Remove your:

- Feelings
- Emotions
- Self

Nobody "feels" like loving their enemies. And sometimes, we do not necessarily "feel" like loving our wives. This is proof that, truly, love is a verb, an action. But what needs to be instilled in us to carry out that command?

- Jesus living inside of you.
- The application of God's Word!
- The ability to see through spiritual eyes.

How you "feel" will not always line up with scripture. You have to view things through spiritual eyes to have an understanding of agapé love and how to put it in action!

Jesus tells us to love our enemies, but you cannot even love your wife?! C'mon, man!

Continuing the construction of the marriage house:

- Best Friend
- Lover
- Unconditional God-like Love

Remember: We want to build a love mansion; not a love shack, baby! (You can thank me later for putting that song in your head!)

On a scale of 1-10, rank how well you apply these loves in your marriage:

_____ She is my best friend and I love being with her.

_____ Our physical intimacy (holding hands, cuddling, kissing, and sex) are awesome!

_____ I love my wife even when she is not lovable.

How would your marriage look if these numbers were higher?

Are you ready to get working?! Let's roll!

FEELINGS... WHOA, WHOA, WHOA, FEELLINGS

Considering we just learned about unconditional love, let's take a deeper dive into this topic. It is something you must have control over to be a Godly Strong husband.

There are going to be things in this devotional that are going to cause you to respond with, "I am not like that," or, "I do not feel like doing that." There will be times your heart is "just not in it," or you may think, "that is just not who I am."

If you want to be who God has called you to be as a Godly Strong husband, you have to master the art of not responding or making decisions based on your feelings and emotions. Learning how to do this will catapult your growth exponentially! There is a reason this process is called, "growing pains!"

Is this easy? No. Is it possible? Absolutely! And the rewards are immense!

All the emotional butterflies and starry eyes are important, no doubt. But those things are byproducts of doing marriage the right way. And what way is that? Loving by action, not emotion.

In other words, you do not love your wife based on how you feel; you love your wife <u>regardless</u> of how you feel!

The following scripture tells us exactly why actions (according to God's Word) trump emotions.

Jeremiah 17:9

*The heart is deceitful above all things and
beyond cure. Who can understand it?*

Why would you want to base the way you love your wife on something that is so deceitful? This is precisely why God gave us His Word; so, we can be guided by what He said instead of guided by our flaky emotions.

Let's check out a story where we see how Jesus handled His emotions and what He did about it.

Matthew 26:36, 42, 44

36 Going a little farther, he fell with his face to the ground and prayed, "My Father, if it is possible, may this cup be taken from me. Yet not as I will, but as you will."

42 He went away a second time and prayed, "My Father, if it is not possible for this cup to be taken away unless I drink it, may your will be done.

44 So he left them and went away once more and prayed the third time, saying the same thing.

Jesus, as shown here THREE times in eight verses, did not "feel" like dying. What was more important to Him was doing what His Father wanted; not what HE wanted.

This is agapé love. The conditions Jesus faced were brutal, and He knew it. But He loved us so much that He put His love for the Father in action instead of being swayed by His emotions.

That is the very mindset you need to have as you progress through this book. This is about fulfilling the purpose God has given you to be a Godly Strong husband.

So… toughen up, big boy and get ready for the ride!

CHALLENGE QUESTIONS

What would have happened if Jesus made His decision based on His emotions instead of God's instructions?

How did He overcome His feelings?

How can you overcome your feelings to ensure you are doing God's will?

What obstacles may hold you back from achieving this?

How can you overcome those obstacles?

The Godly Strong Challenge

Control your emotions! Begin getting in the mindset that your feelings can sometimes deceive you and lead you in the wrong direction.

Furthermore, start working on strategies to help you do the right thing regardless of what your emotions tell you to do.

YES, YOU'RE HONORED!

Have you ever heard someone say, "Man, Satan HATES it when a church is on fire during those services!" Would you believe, in a sense, he's NOT worried about that?!

What if you were told Satan's prime target was not the church? Why? He really does not care what happens there because, unfortunately, what happens there stays there.

All Satan must do in order to destroy the church is destroy marriages. Not only that, but considering marriage is supposed to reflect Christ and the church, what better way to distort that view to the world than wreaking havoc on marriages? The question then becomes, "How do we prevent that from happening?" Our answer begins with the following scripture.

Hebrews 13:4

Marriage is to be held in honor among all, and the marriage bed is to be undefiled; for God will judge the sexually immoral and adulterers.

This verse is the baseline for marriage. Everything you do as a husband must be weighed against this scripture. Every choice you make, everywhere you go, your conduct, your attitude, and even your kids must be measured against this verse.

This simple verse tells us to honor our marriage and if we do that, the marriage bed remains pure, sexual immorality does not happen, and adultery is not on the radar. You know, the law of order! But how do we do that? What does it really mean?

We will take many dives into the Strong's Greek Lexicon to check out Greek and Hebrew words throughout to get a better understanding. We will start with this verse.

Strong's Greek Lexicon

HONOR

Greek Word: Timios (tim'-ee-os)

Definition: Valued, precious

Expanding on that definition and checking out the metaphoric meaning gives us a lot of insight on just how to honor your marriage.

Figuratively: Held in honor, esteemed (respected and admired), and especially dear.

You must recognize the value of your marriage as God sees it. This takes an awakening and an opening of your spiritual eyes.

But then you say, "If you just knew how my wife was, you would realize how difficult that is."

Yeah, maybe so, but check this out…

Romans 5:8

God demonstrated His own love for us in this; while we were still sinners, Christ died for us.

Notice the "when" of this scripture. "While we were still sinners."

To reiterate: The Greek word for sinner (or sin) describes this as someone who has "missed the mark." If you feel as if your wife is "missing the mark," remember Romans 5:8.

Christ did that very thing for you, but you cannot love your wife because of "how she is?" Thankfully, Jesus did not have that attitude toward YOU! So, how did HE respond instead?

1 John 4:19

We love because he first loved us.

He took the first step in recognizing the value in His bride. He did not wait until we got our stuff together to love us. He did that "while" we were in drunken stupors, practicing sexual immorality, lying, cheating, stealing, and quite literally were His enemy. Yet, He loved us FIRST. Maybe apply that to your wife instead of complaining about her!

Here is another idea... maybe pray for her and spend your energy on that instead?

The Godly Strong Rhema Translation

Romans 5:8

But the husband demonstrates his own love for his wife in this; while his wife can be unlovable and miss the mark at times, he still lays his life down for her every day.

How is that for an example?!

SIDENOTE: We are not talking about major issues like abuse and adultery here because that is on another level. We are talking

16

about practical living scenarios. Those things at higher levels need to be addressed with a Christian marriage counselor/coach and/or your pastor.

Let's take a look at some other scriptures where timios can be found for some emphasis:

---

1 Peter 1:18-19

18 For you know that it was not with perishable things such as silver or gold that you were redeemed from the empty way of life handed down to you from your ancestors,

19 but with <u>precious</u> (timios) blood, as of a lamb unblemished and spotless, the blood of Christ.

If His blood is timios, what does that say about marriage which is to be held in timios?

If Satan can distort how precious (timios) marriage is, then how will the world view the preciousness of His redeeming blood? See the common theme here?

Let's bring this home!

In the following "Godly Strong Rhema Translation," write your wife's name in the blank.

The Godly Strong Rhema Translation

Hebrews 13:4

" _Catherine_ _is to be held in honor,
esteemed, and especially dear among all._

The bottom line?

When you honor your wife, you honor God.

When you dishonor your wife, you dishonor God.

CHALLENGE QUESTIONS

_____ On a scale of 1-10, how accurate is that Godly Strong Rhema Translation where your wife's name is written? ?

What can you do to increase that number?

What are your takeaways from what you just learned?

The Godly Strong Challenge:

Even if you feel like you are already prioritizing your wife, find ways to increase how you value her and take it up another level! And if you are not valuing her? NO! EXCUSES! Get on it!

Remember, honoring God is our priority, so as you work on the things to honor your wife, remember that ultimately, you are honoring (or dishonoring!) God in how you value her. Not only is she your wife, but she is His precious daughter, His treasure.

"Yes, my wife, you're HONORED!"

CUT IT OUT!

Remember those "growing pains" mentioned earlier? Here we go! You just might be shocked to learn about someone else who experienced this very thing, and He did not even do anything wrong! But for us? Sometimes, hard knocks are what it takes for us to "get it."

Every day we have choices to make. Every choice has a consequence and too many times, we make the wrong choice. In return, we suffer negative consequences. Why is it so hard for us to just do the right thing? How do we get to the point where doing the right thing is the main priority? The answer is G-R-O-W-T-H! to be who you are called to be as a husband, you must grow as a man, and as a Christian. When you do that, everybody around you flourishes, including your wife.

We now pick up on Jesus talking to the disciples…

John 15:1-4

1 "I am the true vine, and my Father is the gardener.

2-A He cuts off every branch in me that bears no fruit…

Wait a minute! Did Jesus just say He has branches that bear no fruit?!

Double take:

John 15:2

*He cuts off every branch in me that bears no fruit,
while every branch that does bear fruit he prunes
so that it will be even more fruitful.*

Yes, that is what He said!

If Jesus, the King of Kings, a man who walked perfectly has branches that bore no fruit and God cut them off, then what makes you think you are above that? C'mon man, let's not be arrogant to the point we think we have it so under control we do not need pruning for growth.

That verse continues:

*"while every branch that does bear fruit he
prunes so that it will be even more fruitful."*

So far, what do we have in this passage?

- Branches that bear no fruit.
- Branches that do bear fruit.

Each of these types of branches will receive some type of consequence, and the action taken depends on the fruit production they offer. We will get to the first type of branch later, but let's take a look at the latter branch.

*"while every branch that does bear fruit he
prunes so that it will be even more fruitful."*

Strong's Greek Lexicon

PRUNING

Greek Word: Thairó (kath-ah'-ee-ro)

Definition: to cleanse

Part of Speech: Verb (an ongoing action!)

Usage: I cleanse, purify, prune.

From Help's Word-Studies:

Make clean by purging (removing undesirable elements); eliminating what is fruitless by purifying (making unmixed).

You see, this is part of being a human. Not all our branches are good. For those bad branches, they need pruned, and that is what this book is all about! It is designed to expose "undesirable elements" so they can be removed, and to validate the good branches so they can grow and be more fruitful.

In other words, our growth and sustainability of that growth is an ongoing process. If you are not producing good fruit, that means too many weeds are choking you, and likely your wife, too!

What is the key to producing good fruit?

---

4 Remain in me, as I also remain in you. No branch can bear fruit by itself; it must remain in the vine. Neither can you bear fruit unless you remain in me.

5 "I am the vine; you are the branches. If you remain in me and I in you, you will bear much fruit; apart from me you can do nothing.

What is the reason for bearing good fruit?

8 This is to my Father's glory, that you bear much fruit, showing yourselves to be my disciples.

With all of this pruning in mind, you now get two choices:

1. You get cut.

Matthew 7:19

Every tree that does not bear good fruit is cut down and thrown into the fire

OR...

2. You get cut.

John 15:2

Every branch that does bear fruit He prunes (cuts back) so it can be more fruitful!

Each one has a specific consequence:

*   Get cut down.
*   Get cut to grow.

Regardless of which one you choose; you are going to get cut!

So, which choice cut will it be?

Because bearing good fruit brings God glory:

Can the way you treat your wife bring God glory?

_____ Yes

_____ No

Does the way you currently treat your wife bring God glory?

_____ Yes

_____ No

_____ Sometimes

Why or why not?

List your "undesirable elements."

What are the consequences of these elements?

The Godly Strong Challenge

Of the things you listed, begin working on your growth in these areas. If you are brave, tell your wife what you are doing and allow her to help you because it is pretty much guaranteed she has noticed them anyway! Her helping you will bless her, and you, too!

ARE YOU YOKING?!

Have you ever heard someone say the Old Testament is irrelevant? Or that we need to focus more on the New Testament rather than the Old Testament? If that is the case, someone should have told Jesus and Paul because both frequently quoted scriptures out of the Old Testament.

While Paul was an expert in the Old Testament law, Jesus always had a "catch" when He quoted the Old Testament scriptures. What was that "catch?" Well, here is an example:

Matthew 5:43-45

43 "You have heard that it was said, 'Love your neighbor and hate your enemy.'

Here, Jesus quotes Leviticus 19:18. But Jesus always had a, well, BUT!

---

44 But I tell you, love your enemies and pray for those who persecute you,

45 that you may be children of your Father in heaven...

His "but" was always followed by a challenge to live at a higher level; to take your walk to the supernatural realm of agapé love.

(For more examples of these challenges in Matthew 5, you can read verses 21-22, 27-28, 31-32, 33-37, and 38-42.)

He does this same thing in the following passage:

Matthew 19:4-6

4 "Haven't you read," he replied (talking to the Pharisees), "that at the beginning the Creator 'made them male and female,' {Genesis 1:27}

5 and said, 'For this reason a man will leave his father and mother and be united to his wife, and the two will become one flesh' {Genesis 2:24}

In this story, Jesus is answering the Pharisees RIDICULOUS question of, "Is it lawful to divorce your wife for any and every reason?" (Matthew 19:3)

Instead of answering them with a "yes or no," which will be explained in a later devotional, He starts in verse four with His answer of how God designed marriage:

- He created them male and female (v.4)
- Quotes Genesis 2:24 (v.5)

Then, as per usual, takes it up another level after quoting an Old Testament scripture!

---

6 So they are no longer two, but one flesh. Therefore what God has joined together, let no one separate.

Dear Pharisees (and those who might be looking for a way out of marriage), your question has been answered!

So, what does "joined together" indicate?

Strong's Greek Lexicon

JOINED

Greek Word: Suzeugnumi (sood-zyoog'-noo-mee)

Definition: To yoke together

Suzeugnumi is derived from the two Greek words:

Greek words	Sýn	Zeúgos
Definition	Identified with	Yoked

When that word is used in the New Testament, it is only in the marriage context. Let me repeat that:

IT IS ONLY USED IN THE MARRIAGE CONTEXT! Not parents, not kids, not grandkids, not any other human relationship other than marriage!

Now, let's dig!

Expanded meaning from the Help's Word-Studies:

- *Jointly yoked.*
- *Yoked (paired together).*
- *When God joins two people together for one purpose*
- *"a union in which a husband and wife live better for the Lord together, than either would do alone."*

There is no such thing as "distantly yoked!" God expects – and commands - you and your wife to be attached to each other. Shall we say, "joined at the neck?!" That closeness allows you to carry out God's purpose TOGETHER.

Just like anything we do, it is to glorify God. But marriage is also to help you walk closer with Jesus with the help of this covenant union and is also there for you both to achieve a purpose.

The Godly Strong Rhema Translation

Matthew 19:6-A

"Therefore, God has closely paired you to your wife for a purpose ..."

Powerful, huh?

Because God jointly paired us with our wives, it means we are joined to her with a divine closeness. If that is not what is happening in your marriage, it is because the flesh has gotten in the way and your marriage is not operating within its design.

We will visit the second half of this verse later.

What do you take away from the fact that this Greek word is only used in the marriage context?

What do you feel is the unified purpose of you and your wife?

_____ On a scale of 1-10, how "closely yoked" to your wife are you?

How can you get closer and more "yoked together?"

How many hours per week do you spend quality time with your wife with no cell phone and no distractions?

_____ out of 168 total hours per week?

How can you increase that?

The Godly Strong Challenge

Talk to your wife about your "one purpose." Then strategize what needs to begin taking place for that to happen.

Additionally, determine if you are living better for Jesus together than you would alone. If not, discuss how to make that happen and get rolling!

ORDER IN THE COURT!

Before we head to the second half of Matthew 19:6, we are going to explore Genesis 2:24 since Jesus mentioned it in verse 5 of Matthew 19.

So, imagine this:

Your anniversary is approaching, and you want to get your wife a nice gift. You know exactly what you want and head to your favorite online shopping website. You click on the "proceed to checkout" button, then select the "confirm order" button. After doing this, you begin searching for that perfect gift you have in mind. You then enter your credit card number, and once you do that, you then add the gift to your shopping cart to purchase the item. Mission accomplished! Wait, It's not? Why?

You cannot purchase something if you have not put the item in the shopping cart! Nobody does it in that order, right? That would be, well, stupid.

God gives us an order and a way to do things because it is best; yet we still want to do it our way, and it just does not work like that. and when it doesn't, we can't figure out why. Go figure!

When you look at how Paul instructed the church in 1 Corinthians 14, He mentioned being in order... twice. One of those verses we have already mentioned, but let's do it again as a refresher, so we can dig down a little bit into it.

1 Corinthians 14:33

*For God is not a God of disorder but of peace—
as in all the congregations of the Lord's people.*

1 Corinthians 14:40

*But everything should be done in a fitting and
orderly way.*

Strong's Greek Lexicon

DISORDER

Greek Word: Akatastasia (ak-at-as-tah-see'-ah)

Definition: Instability

We will not dig into this word as much as others, but the expanded meaning is:

"Commotion", which generates confusion (things being "out of control"). This uncertainty inevitably generates more instability.

If the above describes any part of your life, then you can bet something is out of order. Marriage's experience this on a consistent basis. The more Satan can get you out of your role, create confusion, and cause disorder, the weaker your marriage is going to be. When your marriage is in order, it will thrive because you are doing it God's way.

The two Biblical principles you learned about earlier – the "law of order" and "the law of first mention" – both can be found in Genesis 2:24.

Not only does this verse has both of these biblical principles, It also has a figurative and literal meaning in it! You could say this verse is loaded! So, let's get to it!

Genesis 2:24

For this reason, a man shall leave his father and his mother, and be joined to his wife; and they shall become one flesh.

This is the first time we see God giving instructions on "how" to be married, and it is in the order He wants it done!

Let's attack this scripture in four parts to understand more what God wants out of our marriage, and how He wants us to approach it.

Genesis 2:24-A

For this reason,...

It is probably a wise idea to learn "the reason" before moving forward. So, what reason?

Genesis 2:23

The man said, "This is now bone of my bones and flesh of my flesh; she shall be called 'woman,' for she was taken out of man."

Notice that Adam was created from dirt; yet Eve was created from Adam? It is one of the most beautiful marriage scriptures in the entire Bible.

Your wife is "bone of your bones and flesh of your flesh;" but sometimes, husbands treat their wives as if they were the ones created from the dirt. Not cool!

"For this reason," could be translated:

"By God's design…"

Law of First Mention

The husband-and-wife team – by God's design – is the primary relationship of all relationships as it was the first human relationship ever created.

Law of Order

The first thing we must do to have a God-purposed marriage is to recognize He is the one who designed it, and if we do it His way – in order - it works!

Additionally, because God created and designed marriage, it is a holy covenant and not a contract. When you said, "I do," and God supernaturally "joined you to your wife," He signed that holy covenant in blood.

The Godly Strong Rhema Translation Part 1

"By God's design…"

CHALLENGE QUESTIONS

What is the difference between a contract signed in ink, and a covenant signed in blood?

How does that apply to your marriage?

The Godly Strong Challenge

Your marriage certificate was signed in ink by the one who was licensed to marry you.

Your marriage covenant was signed in blood by the one who supernaturally joined you.

Do you value your marriage as a blood covenant or a crayon covenant?

Your challenge is to recognize the significance of this blood signature. Remember Hebrews 13:4 and how "precious" marriage is to God. His "blood" is also precious, and that blood was used on your marriage certificate!,

It is time to treat your marriage as a valued treasure!

HAVE YOU LOST YOUR BEHIND?!

Genesis 2:24

For this reason, a man shall leave his father and his mother, and be joined to his wife; and they shall become one flesh.

There are a few different ways you can "lose your behind."

Maybe you entered a business deal that did not work, so you "lost your behind" financially.

Maybe you wanted to lose some weight and your actual goal WAS to lose (some of) your behind!

Maybe you feel like you have also "lost your behind" because you got married. But maybe, just maybe, losing your behind is a good thing!

Genesis 2:24-B

... a man shall leave his father and his mother...

If you are a careful observer, you might have noticed that Adam and Eve had no "father and mother" to leave. So, what is the point here?

Because – as mentioned previously - marriage is the first recorded human relationship (law of first mention), it is the baseline for all other human relationships. That means…

- Marriage takes precedence over all other human relationships.
- It is foreshadowing that a major marriage issue could be parents sticking their noses where they do not belong, or kids that might still depend on you when they are also married.
- Implicates us to create boundaries around the husband and wife team.
- Promotes uniqueness and exclusiveness of the marriage covenant.
- Instructs us to leave our old lives behind for our new life.

To emphasize these points, let's break down what the word "leave" means.

Strong's Hebrew Lexicon

LEAVE

Hebrew Word: Azab

Definition: To leave, forsake, loose

The Literal Meaning

For those still living at home and about to embark on this new life called marriage, it literally means, "Leave your mommy and daddy!"

Support yourself, forsake your dependence upon them, and cut the umbilical cord!

Just because you move out does not mean you have left home! Does this describe you, "Mr. Husband? If so, your wife wants a man; not a little boy.

Oh, and if you are a parent? For your child to "leave father and mother," you have to LET! THEM! GO!

Prov 22:6

Start children off on the way they should go, and even when they are old they will not turn from it.

The way they should WHAT?! GOOOOOO!

The Figurative Meaning

Not all of us are able to literally "leave our father and mother." Some have been divorced; some have been widowed; some have already moved out, etc. Regardless of the reason, we have to apply a lost art in reading the Word, and that lost art is "common sense."

Figuratively, "father and mother" means to abandon "your old life." Whether you are leaving your parents or leaving your single life, it is the same principle.

Let's now head back to Matthew 19:5 where Jesus was quoting Genesis 2:24 and learn what Greek word He used and its meaning.

Strong's Greek Lexicon

LEAVE

Greek Word: Kataleipó (kat-al-i'-po)

Definition: to leave, leave behind

Expanding on this from the Thayer's Greek Lexicon:

"To forsake, leave to oneself a person or thing, by ceasing to care for it, to abandon, leave in the lurch."

Turn on your common sense monitor quickly! This is not saying to "not care for" your parents if that is what you are leaving when you get married. That home is just not your priority any longer and all of your focus is to be on your new home, with your new wife, with your new life.

What part of your old, single life have you not abandoned?

- Checking out other women? **STOP!**
- Taking out things on your wife because of what your ex did? **STOP!**
- Hanging out with others (besides your wife) as much as you did before you were married? **STOP!**
- Playing hours upon hours of video games (not spending much time with your wife)? **STOP!**
- Think the world revolves around you? **STOP!**

Trying to take your old life and fit it into your new one is a recipe for disaster. The old and the new do not mix!

Mark 2:21-22

21 "No one sews a patch of unshrunk cloth on an old garment. Otherwise, the new piece will pull away from the old, making the tear worse.

22 And no one pours new wine into old wineskins. Otherwise, the wine will burst the skins, and both the wine and the wineskins will be ruined. No, they pour new wine into new wineskins."

The Godly Strong Rhema Translation Part 2

*By God's design a man shall **leave behind** his old life...*

CHALLENGE QUESTIONS

What things from your past are causing issues in your marriage?

What can you do to set boundaries around those things?

The Godly Strong Challenge

Establish boundaries around those things you are limiting (shall we say, pruning?!) so they do not grow back up as weeds and choke your marriage to death!

"HOT PURSUIT! KEW, KEW, I LOVE IT, I LOVE IT!"

Genesis 2:24

For this reason a man shall leave his father and his mother, and be joined to his wife; and they shall become one flesh.

What comes to mind when you hear the word, "pursuit?"

One of the best TV characters of all time was Rosco P. Coltrane; the goofy sheriff from The Dukes of Hazzard. This is not debatable, so do not try! Who knew one of his famous phrases would end up in a husband's expanded devotional?!

So far, we have:

- Recognizing that God designed marriage.
- Leave your old life.

That is step 2 of 4; now on to the third!

Genesis 2:24-C

And unite to his wife...

Strong's Hebrew Lexicon

UNITE

Hebrew Word: Dabaq (daw-bak')

Definition: To cling, cleave, keep close.

As you know, a verb is an action. This scripture tells us to "unite" to the wife, and here is what that means according to the Word of God.

- *Cling (like a pesky dryer sheet)*
- *Keep close (so nothing can come between you)*
- *Fasten its grip*
- *Hold tight*

Figuratively to "catch by pursuit"

When dating, what do we do? We "pursue" our "girlfriend" because we want to make them happy and be great for them in a variety of ways.

We attend things with them we do not like; we talk on the phone for hours after texting with them all day; we prioritize them and do what it takes just to be in their presence.

There is nothing wrong with that; however, we stop when we get married when scripture teaches us otherwise. Notice who it says to "catch by pursuit?" It says, the WIFE! Not girlfriend; not fiancé, but WIFE! We have it backwards!

"But life is." just STOP. No excuses. PURSUE HER!

Pursuing your wife cultivates emotional intimacy. Women especially – in general - are very emotional beings, so why would you not want to be a part of that? There are parts of your wife that can only be fulfilled by you unless the wife goes out of bounds and sins. God tells you – not requests you – to pursue her to help fulfill that part of her emotional needs. If this is something you are not doing, you are absolutely in disobedience to His Word.

Let's move to Matthew 19:5 and look at the Greek word Jesus used when He quoted Genesis 2:24.

Strong's Greek Lexicon

UNITE

Greek Word: Kollaó (kol-lah'-o)

Definition: To glue, unite

This is a reflexive verb. That means, in this context, you can word it like this:

I join myself closely, cleave, adhere (to), I keep company (with).

Notice how you are the one causing yourself to "join yourself closely?"

God "joins you together" in the marriage covenant. It is up to you to "continue the hot pursuit" in order for it to stay that way. Otherwise, separation can start developing without even recognizing it.

From Help's Word-Studies:

Kollaó comes from the word, "kólla" which means: glue") – to bond (cleave), adhere to (literally, "glued together"); to cleave, join to.

Figuratively: Intimately connected in a soul-knit friendship.

THAT, my friend, is just how close God wants you and your wife to be figuratively and literally. It is your responsibility to do what you can to have that type of a close knit intimacy with her. If you are not as close as this scripture tells you to be, do not let it be because of you!

42

Therefore, step 3 of 4 is to learn how to pursue someone other than yourself. And, in this case, that someone else is your wife!

The Godly Strong Rhema Translation Part 3

> *By God's design a man shall **leave behind** his old life, catch his wife by hot pursuit, hold her tight and glue himself to her...*

CHALLENGE QUESTIONS

With "hotly pursuing" in mind, name some things you did for your wife when you dated whether it is dating activities, things you did for her "just because," etc.

Out of the things you listed, how many of them do you still do?

_____ On a "sweetness" level, on a scale of 1-10, how did you talk to her when you dated?

_____ On a "sweetness level," on a scale of 1-10, how do you talk to her now?

When are you going to return to pursuing her like you did when you dated?

The Godly Strong Challenge:

Be an imitator of Roscoe when he would exclaim, "I'm in HOT PURSUIT! Kew, kew… I love it, I love it!"

If you are pursuing, make it a hot pursuit. If you are not pursuing, it is time to start the engine, turn on the lights, and get moving!

Review all of the items above and begin implementing those things in your marriage to the level they were when you dated.

NOTE: This has NOTHING to do with sex! But it could definitely lead to it! Just do not let that be your motivation!

Begin pursuing her by dating, leaving notes around the house on occasion, doing something special for her even If it's a "small thing" like picking up her favorite snack on the way home from work. Something simple to say, "I love you," without even having to say it! But then, um, say it!

Or, how about simply looking her in the eyes and listening to her when she talks? Those types of things will do wonders for her, even if it is not noticeable!

Oh, and here is an idea! Those things you used to do when you dated. Do it! (Providing it is not against God's Word, of course!)

The pursuit of the wife NEVER stops. You are to be connected to her emotionally; being romantic partners as well as best friends.

Scripture instructs us to learn how to pursue someone other than ourselves, and your wife is the prime target of pursuit according to Genesis 2:24 and Hebrews 13:4!

One thing about Rosco; he never stopped his pursuit of the Duke boys. His problem was that when he caught them, he would let his guard down and they would get away because he stopped paying attention. Do not let that be you!

OH YEAH, BABY!

Genesis 2:24

For this reason, a man shall leave his father and his mother, and be joined to his wife; and they shall become one flesh.

The final piece of the marriage puzzle in principle is here! Oh, and you are going to love it!

- By God's design...
- You leave your old life...
- **And pursue your wife; holding her tight to cultivate emotional intimacy...**

Steps 3 of 4 complete, so here we go!

Genesis 2:24-D

And the two will become one flesh.

Because this is so deep and complex, we need to do some digging into the Hebrew language to fully understand. The word we will now examine is, "flesh." What does "one flesh" really mean in a literal sense?

Strong's Hebrew Lexicon

FLESH

Hebrew Word: Basar (baw-sawr')

this may be difficult to grasp unless you have a theological degree, but at the risk of confusing you, here it is:

Definition: Flesh.

Yep, that is it, flesh!

Other uses of the word in the NASB: Body, person.

- "And they shall become one body."
- "And they shall become one person."

How cool is that?! Powerful, huh?

Let's now follow a paper trail to learn the literal meaning.

In this segment of 1 Corinthians 6 of which you are about to read, Paul is addressing the issue of sexual immorality.

1 Corinthians 6:15-16-A

15 Do you not know that your bodies are members of Christ himself? Shall I then take the members of Christ and unite them with a prostitute? Never!

16 Do you not know that he who unites himself with a prostitute is one with her in body? For it is said, "The two will become one flesh."

When Paul writes, "he who unites himself with a prostitute ," he is talking about having sex with her. In today's world, this is sex outside of marriage, or, "sexual immorality."

Let's now rewind a bit and go back to where Jesus constantly was taking us to higher levels of living. Notice the wording when He would do this:

Matthew 5:38

"You have heard that it was said, 'Eye for eye, and tooth for tooth.'"

"You have heard it was said" is the phrase Jesus used when quoting an Old testament scripture. In this case it was Exodus 21:24. Paul does this same exact thing in the following passage as we read verse 16 in full:

1 Corinthians 6:16

Do you not know that he who unites himself with a prostitute is one with her in body? For it is said, "The two will become one flesh."

And what old testament scripture is he referring to? Yes, Genesis 2:24!

The Literal Meaning

Being Paul was quoting Genesis 2:24 in this passage, and being it was in the context of sex, we can easily conclude "the two shall become one flesh" means just that; sex!

"The two will become one body" …. Literally!

47

Sex is a beautiful gift of God for those within the marriage covenant. Would you also believe it is a form of worship when you are sexually intimate with your wife? This will be explained later, but sex is so much more than just, well, sex. But one thing we can surely take from this is that sex is commanded by God within the marriage covenant.

The Figurative Meaning

Figuratively, Genesis 2:24-D is telling us you are one unit, one team, partners, and unified in life; doing life together; almost like you are operating as, shall we say, one person!

Notice the "law of order" as this verse comes into focus.

1. By God's design (Genesis 2:24-A)
2. Leave behind (Genesis 2:24-B) so you can
3. Have emotional intimacy… (Genesis 2:24-C) So you can…
4. Have physical and sexual intimacy… (Genesis 2:24-D)

A lack of emotional and physical intimacy will kill a marriage. Is there any wonder why God put both of those in one single verse? It is almost like He knows what He is talking about!

Additionally, God wants us to connect in this order for a reason.

When times get tough in marriage, a great sex life is not what helps you get through it together. It is being the best of friends and the emotional connection you have that will help you fight together to overcome. This is why relationships built on sex often fail. There really is no substance.

But when you add the emotional intimacy that is strong, the sex is great, then you can PUT it all together!

- **P**artnership
- **U**nity
- **T**eamwork

48

But just because the mention of sex in marriage is last in the "law of order" does not mean it is any less significant in importance. It just means before you want to ravish your wife, you had better have taken care of the prior step beforehand! Emotional intimacy is a non-negotiable aspect of a great (or greater) sex life!

To get to the emotional and physical intimacy, you have to leave your past behind and create boundaries around your marriage. Otherwise, the emotional and physical areas will suffer. Notice the common theme with emotional and physical intimacy:

To create emotional intimacy, you must pursue, hold her tight, and glue!

To create physical/sexual intimacy, you have to, um, pursue, hold her tight, and glue!

Therefore, if you are holding your wife tight and are glued to her emotionally, there is figuratively no space between you.

If you are holding your wife tight and are glued to her physically/sexually, there is literally no space between you.

What is the theme?

NO SPACE!

This certainly lines up perfectly with being "yoked together" since you cannot be "distantly yoked."

THIS, my friend, is God's design for marriage!

NOTE! Physical intimacy is not always sex. Love on your wife and give her a simple hug. There is no space between you when you hug her, right? Wait... you do not like to hug because that is "not you?" Go back to, "Feelings... Whoa, Whoa, Whoa Feeling."

If you touch her more in a non-sexual way, becoming "one flesh" the way Genesis 2:24 describes might happen more often. Just sayin' …

The Godly Strong Rhema Translation Part 4

Genesis 2:24

By God's design a man shall leave behind his old life, catch his wife by hot pursuit, hold her tight and glue himself to her, and then have sex!

CHALLENGE QUESTIONS

On a scale of 1-10, rate each category of where they were when you dated and where they are now:

Emotional Intimacy

	When Dating	Married
Compliments	_____	_____
Saying "I love you"	_____	_____
Understanding	_____	_____
Valuing Her	_____	_____

Physical Intimacy

	When Dating	Married
Holding Hands	_____	_____
Hugs	_____	_____
Cuddling	_____	_____
Kisses	_____	_____
COLUMN TOTAL	_____	_____

On a scale of 1-10

_____ How much effort do you put into emotional intimacy?

_____ How much effort do you put into physical/sexual intimacy?

Which one is higher?

_____ Emotional   _____ Physical

If Sexual/physical is higher, then what can you do to increase the emotional intimacy?

If either is below 10, what can you do to raise those numbers?

The Godly Strong Challenge

Regarding Genesis 2:24-D

When sex is on your mind, analyze how much effort you put into her emotionally that day/week. If your emotional investment does not match your desire for sexual intimacy, figure out a way to improve that.

Women are generally more emotional than men, so you have to prioritize her above yourself to make sure her needs are also met. This is God's purpose for you, and she is worth it!

The Godly Strong Challenge #2

Somewhat of a continuance of earlier...

In the first rating scale, make it your goal to increase the "married scores" higher than the "when you dated" scores (or at least match it if the dating score is 10).

SPACE INVADERS

Speaking of closeness for those who are married, we will now continue on with Matthew 19:6

Matthew 19:6

"So they are no longer two, but one flesh. Therefore what God has joined together, let no one separate."

We have already learned in this verse that God is the One who has joined marriages together. We are jointly yoked to our wives, they are walking beside us to accomplish a purpose, and we are associated with our wives through marriage.

We also have learned that Genesis 2:24 gives us the appropriate steps, in sequence, to a healthy marriage the way God designed it.

Matthew 19:6-B

"Therefore what God has joined together, let no one separate."

It is common to interpret this verse as saying, "What God has joined together (two people in marriage), let no man separate (they are not to divorce)." Yeah, you can interpret it like that and be accurate, but there is so much more to what Jesus is saying! Are you ready to keep digging?

Strong's Greek Lexicon

SEPARATE

Greek Word: Chorizo (kho-rid'-zo)

Definition: Separate, Divide

Properly: Put asunder, i.e., depart, vacate.

Expanded definition:

To create "space" (which can be very undesirable or unjustified).

Ah oh! Remember that "no space" thing?

It is God's desire for no space of any kind to be between the husband and wife. After all, that is the way He designed it and Jesus backed that up when He said that we are to (figuratively) glue ourselves to the wife! If something is glued together, there is no space there, right? Right!

For a closer look at the word "separate," check out how it is used in scripture:

"I separate," "put apart," "I separate myself," "I depart," "I withdraw."

This word is also a reflexive verb, meaning you are the one making a decision to willingly do something.

So, you could word it like, "I willingly separate myself from."

Are you willingly doing things that are causing tension and separation in your marriage?

But wait! There's more! Here goes Jesus, once again, urging us to take it to another level! What is up with that?

To vacate: Refers to divorcing a marriage partner who vacates the relationship in soul or body (cf. Moulton-Milligan, 696).

Wait, what?! In soul OR body? You can be divorced while still being married!

You see, just because you are married does not mean you have a marriage.

But here is the beauty of scripture right before our very eyes. Watch how this lines up perfectly with Genesis 2:24.

Matthew 19:6

To vacate in "body or soul."

BODY: We know what a body is. It is the physical, fleshly part of us. Genesis 2:24-D tells us to become "one body" with the wife (IE: physical and sexual intimacy).

But what about the soul? What exactly is it?

Strong's Hebrew Lexicon

SOUL

Hebrew Word: Nephesh (neh'-fesh)

Definition: A soul, living being, life, self, person, desire, passion, appetite, emotion

Wait, what is that last word? EMOTION!

What does Genesis 2:24-C tell us to do? It tells us to create emotional intimacy by pursuit of the wife and to glue ourselves to her; hence, the SOUL connection!

Is scripture not beautiful?! Watch this!

Matthew 19:6-B

Let no man SEPARATE (by legal divorce), by soul (emotionally, Genesis 2:24-C), or by body (physically, Genesis 2:24-D).

In plain terms:

- Do not intimately divorce your wife emotionally.
- Do not intimately divorce your wife physically.
- Do not intimately divorce your wife sexually!

You can do all these things without divorcing her legally. So, if you are not emotionally, physically, or sexually connected with your wife, you are in danger of violating God's principles in His design for marriage and you are missing the mark.

There is yet another aspect of this we need to always keep in mind.

Ephesians 4:27

and do not give the devil a foothold.

Strong's Greek Lexicon

FOOTHOLD

Greek Word: Topos

Definition: A place

Hmmm…. And according to Strong's Exhaustive Concordance:

"A spot (general in space, but limited by occupancy."

Once a snake gets its head in an opening, the rest of the body follows. Why do you think it is so important to not have any emotional, physical, or sexual space between you and your wife? Because you are giving the devil "room to move," which is also the definition of "foothold!"

The Godly Strong Rhema Translation

Ephesians 4:27

Do not give the devil a space...

The Godly Strong Rhema Translation (in full)

Matthew 19:6

Therefore, God has closely paired you with your wife for a purpose, so let nothing or no one (including YOU!) create emotional or physical space between you.

CHALLENGE QUESTIONS

In a general sense, list what might be causing space between you and your wife. (Some of these things might not even be initiated by you, but things you can control).

EXAMPLE: Friends constantly calling or texting, visiting, etc.

What type of boundaries can be established to prevent this space from being created? Remember, scripture (Hebrews 13:4) instructs us to value our spouse "among all."

What behaviors do you exhibit (or not exhibit) toward your wife that might be causing division?

How can you correct that?

The Godly Strong Challenge

When you leave your old life, you are attaching yourself to your wife (by God's design). When it is done correctly, there is such a bond emotionally and physically that nothing can get in between you.

But if your space invaders are things such as a bad attitude, lack of attention toward your wife, etc., begin working on turning those things around (and all of those on your list!)!

SOMEONE NEEDS A HEART TRANSPLANT

Let's start this one off by rewinding a little bit to expand on Matthew 19 where the Pharisees were confronting Jesus. It is necessary to learn what the Pharisees were up to for context.

Matthew 19:3

Some Pharisees came to him (Jesus) to test him. They asked, "Is it lawful for a man to divorce his wife for any and every reason?"

They were trying to trick Jesus with this question.

Divorce at that time was about a 5-minute process if that. If you happened to notice an attractive woman and concluded you would rather have her instead of your wife, it did not take much effort to divorce her. All you had to do was get a certificate of divorce, hand it to her, and that was it!

Then, as soon as you served her the certificate, you could walk right over to the girl you had your eye on and marry her, all in "one motion," in a way.

Therefore, if Jesus answered "yes," to their question to "divorce for any reason," the Pharisees would get their approval to continue this appalling behavior.

But if Jesus answered "no," that you could not divorce for "any and every reason," then He would be violating the law of Moses (Deuteronomy 24:1-4).

Regardless of which way He answered, the Pharisees thought they had Him painted into a corner. That is when Jesus answered the way He did in a scripture you will recognize:

Matthew 19:4-6

4 "Haven't you read," he replied (talking to the Pharisees), "that at the beginning the Creator 'made them male and female,' {Genesis 1:27}

5 and said, 'For this reason a man will leave his father and mother and be united to his wife, and the two will become one flesh' {Genesis 2:24}

6 So they are no longer two, but one flesh. Therefore what God has joined together, let no one separate."

Jesus did not answer their trick question. He simply explained to them God's design for marriage.

Of course, the Pharisees just could not help themselves. They kept running their mouths and pressing Jesus to try and get an answer to justify their behavior. That is where we pick up the story.

7 "Why then," they asked, "did Moses command that a man give his wife a certificate of divorce and send her away?"

Again, trying to catch Him going against Moses! But then, Jesus drops the bomb.

8 Jesus replied, "Moses permitted you to divorce your wives because your hearts were hard. But it was not this way from the beginning."

Jesus identifies the problem with divorce and the root cause, and that is the hardness of heart (sin). But what is it that Jesus is saying about a hardened heart, and how does it get this way?

Strong's Greek Lexicon

HEARTS WERE HARD

Greek Word: Sklérokardia (sklay-rok-ar-dee'-ah)

Definition: Hardness of heart

sklérokardia is derived from two Greek words:

Greek Word:	Sklēró	Kardia
Definition:	Hard because dry	Heart

The definition from Help's Word-Studies (hold on to your fannies, fellas!):

An obstinate, hard heart which lacks the oil of the Holy Spirit and hence implies rebellion – I.E someone refusing to be receptive (obedient) to God's inworking of faith.

Yikes! Read it again and let it sink in!

When we lack the oil of the Holy Spirit to fill our hearts through living a consistent Christian life, our heart begins to dry up to the sensitivity of the Holy Spirit to lead us. We can become desensitized and not even know it. Hence, making it very difficult for us to lead our wives and be sensitive to her as well. It takes the leading of the Holy Spirit to be the husband you are called to be and without Him, you are going to struggle like an engine with no oil.

Unfortunately, we do not recognize sometimes that our engine is running a bit rough because it becomes the norm, then BOOM! It quits. You must have a maintenance plan for your marriage, and it starts with you!

The best way to maintain your marriage and cultivate your growth as a husband is to be in the Word of God so that you are sensitive to the Holy Spirit. Otherwise, you very well may dry up!

Evaluate if any of these describe you:

- Obstinate
- Hard heart
- Lacks the oil of the Holy Spirit
- Rebellious (stubbornness)
- Refusing to be receptive to God's inworking of faith.
- Disobedient

How are you going to lead her if you barely know who Jesus is?

How are you going to lead her if your heart is obstinate?

How are you going to lead her if you are not growing in your faith?

How are you going to lead her if your heart is hard?

How are you going to lead her if any of the above bullet points are part of your character?

Matthew 19:8

Jesus replied, "Moses permitted you to divorce your wife because of your disobedience as well as your Refusal to be receptive to God's inworking of faith, and because your heart lacked the oil of the Holy Spirit. But it was not this way from the beginning."

One sure way to create separation from your wife emotionally and physically is to not be in tune with God and His direction; to make marriage about you and not her. Get out of your own way (and God's!), prioritize your wife, and prioritize your walk with the Designer of marriage Himself!

Sin separates us from God, and also separates us from our wives. That qualifies as "missing the mark!"

Rank how the description of a hard heart in the bullet points above applies to you on a scale of 1-10:

_____ Obstinate

_____ Hard heart

_____ Lacks the oil of the Holy Spirit

_____ Rebellious (stubbornness)

_____ Refusing to be receptive to God's inworking of faith.

_____ Disobedient

_____ On a scale of 1-10, How much do you depend on scripture to help you lead your wife?

Who is leading you in your marriage?

___ The Holy Spirit   ___ Me   ___ My wife _____ Nobody

Who is the spiritual leader in your marriage?

___ The Holy Spirit   ___ Me   ___ My Wife ___ Nobody

What needs to change, if anything, in the last two questions?

The Godly Strong Challenge

Take a closer look at the bullet points and how you ranked yourself. These are all things that describe a hardened heart.

One at a time, begin working on improving each item. And remember it all starts with watering your heart with the Living Water and the oil of the Holy Spirit!

Therefore, get yourself on a consistent, daily schedule to continue oiling your heart by God's Word and prayer!

Prayer and Reading Schedule

Monday: ___:___ AM/PM

Tuesday: ___:___ AM/PM

Wednesday: ___:___ AM/PM

Thursday: ___:___ AM/PM

Friday: ___:___ AM/PM

Saturday: ___:___ AM/PM

Sunday: ___:___ AM/PM

STOP HAVING AN AFFAIR!

What? You are not having an affair? Hmm... let's see about that.

We just learned that Jesus said we are to have no space in our marriage. Sometimes, those things can creep in that cause division without us even noticing. That is why we always need to be alert and recognize when that happens. But what about those things we knowingly do?

Before we address that, let's do a quick review:

Genesis 2:24 tells us to hold tight and glue ourselves to our wives, right? Right!

Hebrews 13:4 tells us that marriage is to be held in honor among all, right? Right!

Matthew 19:6 says that God has joined you to your wife which means you are yoked to her, right? Right!

And Matthew 19:6 also says, because God has joined you together, to let no one separate that covenant union, right? Right!

So, what, according to scripture, is to be your priority? Your marriage and wife, right? Right!

Now that we have that established, let's head to the book of Jeremiah where we see a disturbing trend of behavior.

Jeremiah 3:6, 8

*6 During the reign of King Josiah, the Lord said
to me, "Have you seen what faithless Israel has
done? She has gone up on every high hill and
under every spreading tree and has committed
adultery there.*

*8 I gave faithless Israel her certificate of divorce
and sent her away because of all her adulteries...*

The "adultery" committed here is the fact Israel was "faithless."
Why? Israel was putting other gods before the almighty God! He
was not their priority; He was not their focus. What belonged #1 in
their hearts dropped down the list to a secondary position, if that.

Jeremiah 3:9

*Because Israel's immorality mattered so little to
her, she defiled the land and committed adultery
with stone and wood.*

What is adultery?

- Literally committing (sexual) adultery.
- Figurative of idolatress worship, which this scripture
  indicates.

Idolatress worship is putting things in front of what rightfully
belongs there. You might not be "worshipping" people or things by
bowing your knees and chanting bizarre things, but if you are
putting other things or people above your wife, that is figurative idol
worship.

Selfishness is also a type of idolatry!

The interesting thing about this is how God used the marriage analogy when He could have used many others.

Isaiah 54:5-8

For your Maker is your husband — the Lord Almighty is his name...

What do you think the purpose would be of God using the analogy of a marriage covenant? Likely to heavily and continually emphasize the rightful place of a spouse. After all, we are the bride of Christ, right?

Additionally, when we head to the new testament, there are other scriptures that talk about adultery in a non-sexual way as well.

James 4:4

You adulterous people, [An allusion to covenant unfaithfulness]. Don't you know that friendship with the world means enmity against God? Therefore, anyone who chooses to be a friend of the world becomes an enemy of God.

So, adultery sometimes includes sexual sin, but also includes "covenant unfaithfulness."

One way to begin the process of becoming an enemy of your wife is to prioritize other things and people above her, and that includes yourself. Your wife becoming your enemy may be an insidious process, but a process nonetheless. Operating in this way gives the devil "room to move" in your marriage because you are out of order.

Remember, your marriage is not a contract (signed in pen); it is a covenant (signed in blood). Therefore, putting anything above your spouse is covenant unfaithfulness and is considered adultery.

What have you taken and moved to the top of the priority list in place of your wife? Or, let's ask it this way: what or who or who are you having an affair with?

The Godly Strong Rhema Translation

Jeremiah 3:9

Because your immorality mattered so little to you, you defiled the marriage (and marriage bed) and committed adultery with (whatever/whomever is taking place of your wife).

What is your "stone and wood?"

- Yourself?
- Your job??
- Your video games?
- Your kids?
- Your friends?
- Sports?

Genesis 2:24 gives us God's guidelines for this covenant union. When you prioritize other things or people over your wife that causes separation emotionally and physically, you are not only exhibiting covenant unfaithfulness to your wife, but also to God. Why? Because the marriage covenant is by "God's design."

When you operate in marriage other than God's way, then you are operating by someone else's rules. You figure it out.

CHALLENGE QUESTIONS

List everything, even the good, that takes up your free time whether it be friends, hobbies, etc.

Of the things you listed, estimate the ratio of time and effort you give to it in comparison to the time and effort you give to your wife:

What would it do for your wife if you prioritized her over your list?

If God walked through your front door and judged you based upon how you invest in your wife verses everything else, would He be pleased?

Why or why not?

What is stopping you from making her your priority?

Would God accept that answer?

The Godly Strong Challenge

Begin moving the things out of the way that are taking the place of your wife in your marriage. She deserves the first part of you; not the leftovers.

Then, repent for putting those things above your wife and honor God's design for marriage by putting her at the top of your priority list!

Sidenote: Let's not get stupid. There is nothing wrong with friends, watching your favorite show or sport, etc. But when they are getting more attention from you than your wife, you are on the slippery slope of committing covenant unfaithfulness, AKA: ADULTERY!.

Jesus made a covenant with you and is holding to it. You should do the same with your wife!

IT'S ALL ABOUT THE MONEY! OR IS IT?

You and your wife are at home and she asks, "Would you please go get the clothes out of the washer and put them in the dryer?" Of course, because you are the best husband ever, you do what she asks.

A couple of hours later, your wife goes to get the clothes out of the dryer. You suddenly hear a loud noise that sounds exactly like her voice. The decibel levels coming out of the laundry room reaches over 100 as you hear, "Did you not turn on the dryer?!"

"But baby, you only told me to put the clothes in the dryer. You did not tell me to turn it on."

You got the surface meaning of what she asked, but not the deeper meaning. If this were to ever happen (please tell me it has not!), I am sure your wife would let you know it is quite important to also turn on the dryer. Once you have that bit of information, you now know the "deeper meaning" of what your wife is telling you. This may sound like a silly scenario, but I am sure it has happened…

Likewise, there are too many times we hear a verse quoted so much that we automatically think we know what it means without studying it for ourselves. We might understand the surface of the meaning, but not the depth. The following verse is one of those:

1 Timothy 5:8

Anyone who does not provide for their relatives, and especially for their own household, has denied the faith and is worse than an unbeliever.

Let's roll through a scenario that is not so uncommon.

A husband is working and providing a majority (or all) of the household income for whatever reason. This particular husband believes he is doing his job and that is all he has to do, so he lets his wife do whatever else is needed in the household.

But what about those who might be disabled? What about those who were providing and lost their job? There are a variety of reasons a man may not be able to "financially provide" for his family at no fault of his own. Maybe his career does not pay as well as the career of his wife; therefore, she generates more money for the household than he does. Does that make him worse than an unbeliever? NOPE! The thing is, this scripture goes much, much deeper than that.

Strong's Greek Lexicon

PROVIDE

Greek Word: Pronoeó (pron-o-eh'-o)

Definition: To foresee

Usage: I take thought for beforehand, provide for, practice.

Do you see anywhere where it only mentions "financial provision?" No sir. This is talking about "seeing ahead" and proceeding with caution with your family's best interest in mind. So yes, it could mean financial. You have to work to provide, but what other things are you to provide? Let's continue using the shovel.

From Help's Word-Studies:

Pronoeó comes from the following:

Greek Word:	Pró	Noiéō
Definition:	Before	Think

And here is what we get:

To think (plan) before, showing necessary forethought to act properly (in God's will).

You already know what God's will is for your marriage from our examinations of Hebrews 13:4, Genesis 2:24, and Matthew 19:6.

Now, you must measure everything you do, say, and think against those scriptures. That means "thinking ahead" to the consequences – good or bad – of the way you proceed.

Are you spending money without any forethought to the household expenses you have coming soon and causing financial strain? You are in violation of God's word.

If you still have children at home and not spending <u>quality</u> time with them, providing them the love and discipline they need (and crave) because you are too ornery, lazy, selfish, or a bit of a JERK… you are in violation!

How about the emotional and physical intimacies we already addressed?

By now, you should get the point. It is a must you provide for your family by foreseeing things down the road as the leader. That is what real leaders do; making decisions and giving forethought for the betterment of those he leads. Otherwise, you are just a little boy mentally, running around with no clue…

The Godly Strong Rhema Translation

---

1 Timothy 5:8

Any husband who does not show necessary forethought to act properly for his extended family, but especially for his wife (and kids) spiritually, emotionally, physically, as well as financially, has denied the faith and is worse than an unbeliever.

Name some ways you may potentially be acting worse than an unbeliever?

What are you going to do to correct it?

How can you "foresee" better in your marriage (and family)?

Your takeaways regarding, "It's all about the money, or is it?"

The Godly Strong Challenge

Analyze your actions this week and before making a decision, think ahead to how it will affect your wife. If it could potentially be a negative response, either talk it over with her or just do not do it.

This is a great habit to get into if you have not already!

I NEVER SAW THAT COMING!

I now present you with the opportunity to make a financial investment. In return, I advise you this investment is of little or no risk, and you will receive a great return on your money. Your ears perked up, right? You are likely thinking of what to do with all of that money you are about to receive if this investment is successful.

Within a few short months, the money starts rolling in. Your investment is growing, and life is good. That is, until you realize you are involved in a Ponzi scheme. You have been outwitted.

Actor Kevin Bacon and professional baseball player Sandy Koufax as well as several banks became victims of Bernard "Bernie" Madoff in the largest Ponzi scheme in history. It seemed innocent enough on the surface, but schemers are quite good at creating an illusion to make you think one thing; yet, something else is really going on behind the scenes.

---

2 Corinthians 2:10-11

10 Anyone you forgive, I also forgive. And what I have forgiven—if there was anything to forgive—I have forgiven in the sight of Christ for your sake,

11 in order that Satan might not outwit us. For we are not unaware of his schemes.

In these instructions, Paul was addressing the people regarding someone who had sinned.

Think about your marriage right now and a time where your wife just ticked you off! How did you handle that at that moment? Better yet, how are you handling that today? Are you still holding it against her, or did you forgive her and let it go?

Listen to Paul's instructions regarding this situation.

2 Corinthians 2:6-7

7 Now instead, you ought to forgive and comfort him (the transgressor), so that he will not be overwhelmed by excessive sorrow.

8 I urge you, therefore, to reaffirm your love for him.

Then Paul drops a bomb as to why it is critically important to forgive:

11 ... in order that Satan might not outwit us.

Strong's Greek Lexicon

OUTWIT

Greek Word: Pleonekteó (pleh-on-cek-teh'-o)

Definition: To have more, to overreach, take advantage

When you harbor unforgiveness toward your wife, even the slightest offense, you are giving the enemy of your marriage a foundation to move; a license to operate and giving him access to your marriage.

Satan wants to overreach and take advantage of you and your wife. He is out to destroy you, destroy her, and destroy your marriage. Once he begins dismantling your marriage, your kids will also suffer consequences. Is it worth it to you?

For him to succeed in this, all he needs is your unwillingness to align with God's Word. Part of that is holding unforgiveness toward your wife.

Unfortunately, we expect grace when we mess up; however, we are not near as willing to extend the grace we feel we, ourselves, deserve. If that is your attitude, that would make you a hypocrite!

Lamentations 3:22-23

22 Because of the Lord's great love we are not consumed, for his compassions never fail.

23 They are new every morning; great is your faithfulness.

God is willing to do this for you on a daily basis, but you are unwilling to extend what you have received to your wife? C'mon…

Mark 11:25

And when you stand praying, if you hold anything against anyone, forgive them, so that your Father in heaven may forgive you your sins. "

"Not forgiving someone is like drinking poison and expecting the other person to die." – Nelson Mandella

James 2:13

13 because judgment without mercy will be shown to anyone who has not been merciful. Mercy triumphs over judgment.

Save the "yeah, but" response and turn it into, "yes, I will."

The Godly Strong Rhema Translation

2 Corinthians 2:7-8, 10-11

7 Now instead, you ought to forgive and comfort your wife, so that she will not be overwhelmed by excessive sorrow.

8 I urge you, therefore, to reaffirm your love for her (so go do that NOW!).

10 Anyone you forgive, I also forgive. And what I have forgiven—if there was anything to forgive— I have forgiven in the sight of Christ for your sake,

11 in order that Satan might not take advantage of you. For you are not unaware of his schemes to destroy your marriage.

Regarding James 2:13, which of the two do you extend the most to your wife?

_____ Judgment   _____ Mercy

Time to be bold:

Regardless of how small or large, what things are you holding against your wife?

What will a Godly Strong man do in this situation who loves his wife like Christ loved the church?

What are the benefits to you, your wife, and your marriage of offering forgiveness, mercy, and grace?

SIDENOTE: Sometimes, we need to extend forgiveness to ourselves. Not forgiving ourselves of things like our past – something we eluded to in Genesis 2:24-B - can hold us back in being the husband God has called us to be.

If this is you, these scriptures also apply

From what things do you need to forgive yourself?

The Godly Strong Weekly Challenge

Bernie Madoff was able to scheme his investors by blinding them to reality. Unforgiveness blinds our spiritual eyes and opens the door for Satan to outwit us. Be a man and forgive your wife of whatever you might be holding against her so that your marriage can flourish! Jesus did it for YOU when you did not deserve it, so it is a great idea to extend the same to your wife if there should be any unforgiveness there.

If this is an area where you struggle, ask God to help you forgive like He does. His forgiveness can save you from hell, and your forgiveness might save your marriage. ask God to help you learn to forgive and move forward so you are not the victim of the biggest spiritual Ponzi scheme of all time!

SORRY ABOUT THAT!

Extending forgiveness is sometimes a difficult thing to do. But saying "I'm sorry" might be even more difficult.

Have you ever noticed when we are at the store and we accidentally bump into somebody, our automatic response is usually, "Oops! Sorry about that!" But if we do something to upset our wife, our automatic response sometimes is to try and prove we did not do anything wrong? Or worse, refuse to admit we did? What is the reason for that? What is the reason we do not treat our one-flesh better than that stranger?

Human nature does not want to admit we may have an imperfection. Human nature wants to always be right and hide the flaws. But therein is the problem, the flesh! Men can be too prideful to admit they just might be wrong, especially when it comes to the wife!

How about we look at "I'm sorry," in a different way:

Doesn't it make sense that, if it is so hard to admit fault and say those two healing words, that it would take someone strong to admit their faults? Saying "I'm sorry" is not an admission of weakness; it is a sign of strength.

But it is more than just saying, "I'm sorry." The heart behind those two words is what truly matters.

In scripture, we find two types of sorrows:

- Godly sorrow
- Worldly sorrow

What is the difference?

---

2 Corinthians 7:10

Godly sorrow brings repentance that leads to salvation and leaves no regret, but worldly sorrow brings death.

Therefore, "I'm sorry" by itself means nothing unless it is accompanied by repentance. But what is repentance?

Strong's Greek Lexicon

REPENT

Greek Word: Metanoeó (met-an-o-eh'-o)

Definition: to change one's mind or purpose

We get a great breakdown of this word from the Help's Word-Studies:

Greek Word:	Metá	Noiéō
Definition:	Changed after being with	Think

And this is what you get when you put those together:

"Think differently after."

Two things are required for you to "think differently after," a for the apology to be effective:

- A heart-felt, "I'm sorry." (Emotions)
- A change in behavior. (Action)

84

An apology based on pretense is nothing more than noise. Oh, the arrogance of those who are unwilling to apologize for their wrongs. And if the change of behavior does not accompany the words, the trust and respect you want from your wife just took a massive hit.

If worldly sorrow (or no sorrow at all) brings death, then a repentant, Godly "I'm sorry," brings life!

Benefits of Godly Sorrow:

- Always produces repentance.
- Comes with deep conviction and remorse.
- Displays humbleness and humility; characteristics of Christ!
- Shows strength, and your wife wants a Godly Strong husband!
- Defeats pride.
- Much like forgiveness, it brings healing.
- Shows great leadership skills.
- Cultivates trust.
- Breaks down emotional walls and/or prevents them from being built!
- Cultivates emotional and physical intimacy.
- Cultivates personal growth.
- Brings about change.
- Is sincere.
- Ticks off Satan.
- Pleases God!

On the flip side, refusing to say, "I'm sorry," or just saying it out of pretense produces the opposite effect.

It is impossible to be Godly Strong with worldly apologies.

The Godly Strong Rhema Translation

2 Corinthians 7:10

A husband's Godly sorrow brings a change to his behavior that leads to a stronger marriage, breathing life into his wife. He is not sorry for being sorry. But a husband's worldly sorrow brings division and potential death to the wife's emotions and ultimately, the marriage!

CHALLENGE QUESTIONS

Which most describes your type of apology?

_____ Godly   _____ Worldly

_____ On a scale of 1-10, how difficult is it for you to admit fault?

_____ On a scale of 1-10, how difficult is it for you to say, "I'm sorry?"

If these are difficult for you, what is the reason?

How can you overcome this difficulty?

What would it do for your wife if you were to willingly admit fault and apologize with repentance included?

How will God react if you were to do this with a genuine and sincere heart?

What would He feel about you if you did not?

The Godly Strong Challenge

This week, understand and accept you are simply not perfect. Nobody is. Fasten your grip (see what I did there?) on the fact that it takes and incredibly strong husband to admit wrong and an even stronger man to apologize. Your wife and marriage will be blessed by it!

If you have been one to offer worldly sorrow, right now is a great time to go offer your wife a Godly apology, even if it is apologizing for not apologizing!

Don't forget: Your apology must be accompanied by action!

IF I WEREN'T ME, I'D SURE WANNA BE!

There are two brothers who are 3 and 5 years old playing in the middle of the living room floor. You hear the beautiful sound of the toddler laugh, all while trying to interpret the conversation. It is adorable!

Also in the middle of the living room floor is a mixed variety of toy vehicles; everything from trucks, to fire engines, to police cars, to sports cars, etc. Then, it happens. The 3-year old picks up the fire engine. With him possessing that vehicle, the 5-year old only has 29 other vehicle option. But that simply is not enough. The 5-year-old wants that fire engine! A tug-of-war ensues as they begin screaming at each other.

You have just witnessed the sibling rivalry.

Whether or not you have kids, there is no doubt you have witnessed this behavior. And if you were honest about it, you would admit that we have to fight this exact tendency as adults.

Example: What is the first thing that comes to your mind when I tell you to do the following:

"Submit yourself to your wife."

What immediately crossed your mind? Probably some type of resistance, right? Why is that? Because submitting goes against human nature. You may have even thought, "She is supposed to submit to me; not the other way around!" Again, that is resistance. Oh, and by the way, if you do not think you are expected to submit to your wife, you are wrong. But we will get to that later.

One of the biggest downfalls of humanity is selfishness. We want it our way, when we want it, how we want it, for as long as we want it, and if we do not get it, we cop an attitude, pout, and act like a child at times. Every single one of us has selfish tendencies, even when it goes against God's will.

And then – God forbid – the wife does not give you what you want, then the tug-of-war begins!

We can experience this type of behavior in things as small as deciding where to eat, and things as serious as finances and even sex.

You have just witnessed the spousal rivalry!

So, how should we approach issues with the wife where there is a disconnection of desires?

Philippians 2:3-4

3 Do nothing out of selfish ambition or vain conceit. Rather, in humility value others above yourselves,

4 not looking to your own interests but each of you to the interests of the others.

Do those two verses describe your attitude toward your wife? Do you value her over yourself? Let's find out …

Strong's Greek Lexicon

VALUE

Greek Word: Huperechó (hoop-er-ekh'-o)

Definition: to hold above, to rise above, to be superior

From Help's Word-Studies:

Greek Word:	Hyper	Exo
Definition:	Beyond, above	Have

Here is what we get:

"have beyond, i.e. be superior, excel, surpass" (A-S); to exercise prominence (superiority).

This is what it means to "value" others (your wife) over yourself.

Additionally, Let's take a quick look at the word, "selfish."

Strong's Greek Lexicon

SELFISH

Greek Word: Eritheia (er-ith-i'-ah)

Core definitions:

- *Rivalry*
- *Carnal (worldly) ambition*
- *Acting on selfish ambition regardless of the discord it causes*
- *Places self-interest ahead of what is good for others.*
- *Places self-interest ahead of what the Lord declares right.*

How many of those core definitions characterize your general behavior toward your wife? Have you made her your rival due to your ambition for things to be your way?

Check out what James says about selfishness:

James 3:16

*For where you have envy and selfish (eritheia)
ambition, there you find disorder and every evil
practice.*

Selfishness begins a very ungodly snowball effect! Not only is it demonic but causes things to be out of order!

Strong's Greek Lexicon

DISORDER

Greek Word: Akatastasia █████████████

Evil practice is found there, too!

1 Corinthians 14:33

*For God is not a God of disorder (akatastasia),
but a God of peace ...*

The definition for disorder (akatastasia) is "instability."

When you are selfish in your ways, you not only are creating a rivalry with your wife; you are creating a rivalry with God. Why? God is a God of peace; not of instability (disorder), and selfishness produces disorder and instability. Also, "every evil thing" can be found there, too! If that does not jolt selfishness out of you, then you need to head back to the chapter entitled, "Someone Needs a Heart Transplant."

There is nothing wrong with having your own desires; however, you are no longer single. This is why it is important for you and your wife to work together in order for both to have your desires met. It is a balancing act, but definitely can be done.

Psalm 133:1

How good and pleasant it is when God's people live together in unity!

How beautiful it is when a marriage operates in unity, when a husband and wife put the other first. Selfishness will destroy that beauty.

Romans 8:5

For those who live according to the flesh set their minds on the things of the flesh, but those who live according to the Spirit set their minds on the things of the Spirit.

In this context, flesh is not of God, but walking in the spirit is. "Choose this day whom you will serve."

Strong's Greek Lexicon

FLESH

Greek Word: Sarx (Sarx)

Definition: Flesh

Sarks is generally negative, referring to making decisions (actions) according to self – i.e. done apart from faith (independent from God's inworking). Thus what is "of the flesh (carnal)" is by definition displeasing to the Lord – even things that seem "respectable!"

In short, flesh generally relates to unaided human effort, i.e. decisions (actions) that originate from self or are empowered by self. This is carnal ("of the flesh") and proceeds out of the untouched (unchanged) part of us – i.e. what is not transformed by God.

One last thing about selfishness:

What is your motivation behind what you do? You can appear to be serving, humble, etc. all while having an ulterior motivation to get something out of it. You may be fooling your wife, but you are not fooling God.

Jeremiah 17:10

"I the Lord search the heart and test the mind, to give every man according to his ways, according to the fruit of his deeds."

The Godly Strong Rhema Translation

Philippians 2:3-5

3 Do nothing out of selfish ambition or vain conceit. Rather, in humility hold your wife above yourself,

4 not looking to your own interests but instead, to the interests of your wife.

CHALLENGE QUESTIONS

What things do you consistently do to get your way instead of blessing your wife?

What would it do for her if you took a back seat and did something that interested her; yet, was not of interest to you?

How would you feel in that moment when you see your wife blessed by your unselfishness?

List things your wife loves to do below.

1.

2.

3.

Write down how you are going to focus on those things to make her feel valued.

How selfish was Jesus when He laid down His life for you?

What has He done for you to bless you rather than focusing on Himself?

The Godly Strong Challenge

You just read that God is not a God of disorder. Acting in a selfish way goes against the very nature of God and His peace.

YOU, sir, are going to join her in her activity/hobby/interest/chores! Look for those things that she enjoys, especially those that do not interest you, and take part in them!

Then, write down below how she reacted and what it did for her.

Response:

The Godly Strong Challenge #2

Read Philippians 2:5-8 as this describes Christ's attitude toward His "bride." Then, write down how you can apply this type of character in your marriage and toward your wife. Review these things frequently until it becomes a habit!

When you apply these concepts, there is a great reward! The beginning of Philippians 2:9 says:

> *"Therefore, God exalted Him to the highest place..."*

It is much more beneficial for you for God to exalt you instead of you exalting yourself!

NOTE: There are some things that you have to be the man of the house and make a decision to the contrary of how the wife feels about it. This is not the example we are setting forth in this devotional. This is for those things that are not life altering, bank breaking, non-wise choices.

LESS ATTITUDE, MORE GRATITUDE!

You and your wife decide to take an evening for a date. You get to your favorite restaurant and hold the door for your wife (you BETTER be holding her door!). As she walks through, you notice someone behind her, and you hold the door a little longer for them. They walk RIGHT past you and do not express even a simple "thank you."

What is your reaction when that happens? Frustrating, right? At that point, your flesh is aching to get out from within and say, "You're welcome!" You know you want to… just don't!

Isn't it quite frustrating that you would make the extra effort to do something for someone and they walk past you as if you do not even exist?

If that is rude for a stranger to do, why do we act like it is no big deal when our wife does something for us and we respond the same way?

You might be saying, "I always thank her when she does things for me." Are you sure about that?

What about:

- Cleaning the house?
- Helping the kids with their homework?
- Helping with finances because she works a job, too?
- Cooking dinner, even if it does not taste so good?
- Doing your laundry?
- Being your wife?
- Putting up with your crap?

What we take for granted are the things we expect. When we expect it, we typically do not have an attitude of thankfulness toward it.

What is the importance of thankfulness toward the wife?

1 Thessalonians 5:18

Be thankful in all circumstances, for this is God's will for you who belong to Christ Jesus.

It is actually in God's will to be thankful! And you know what? Your wife needs to hear that from you regularly. Serving someone is doing it without expectation of getting anything in return; however, to not show enough gratitude can even make the strongest of servants deflate and grow weary.

But when you thank your wife for the things that are unexpected, you are breathing life into her and causing her to feel appreciated. This is what a true leader does; ensuring those who are serving in any capacity feel appreciated and desired.

So, do you want to be in God's will or not?

The Godly Strong Rhema Translation

1 Thessalonians 5:18

Be thankful in all circumstances toward your wife, for this is God's will for you who belong to Christ Jesus.

List the ordinary, boring, mundane things your wife does consistently. Bonus points if you hate doing something you list, but do not have to do it because she does it (laundry, anybody?)!

1.

2.

3.

4.

5.

What things on the list have you never (or has been a very long time) thanked your wife for doing?

The Godly Strong Challenge

Make an extra effort to start looking for those things for which you have never thanked your wife. Make a list and then go to her and verbally give her thanks for doing what she does (and make this a HABIT).

You can simply thank her, or find a unique way to thank her for all of the things she does whether it be a card, a rose, a note in her purse that she will find, etc.

You can start with that list above.

BONUS: Do something extra special for her as an act of appreciation.

YOU'RE KILLING ME!

By now, you realize that the wife has the ability to make you angry. Obviously, we do not make them mad at all in our divine perfection (sarcasm!); yet, even when our anger toward the wife might be completely justified, we still have to be very, very careful in our handling of that anger.

God gives us some great instruction on "how" to be angry with the wife without sinning. Before we take a look at that, let's check out what Jesus said about anger:

Matthew 5:21-22

21"You have heard that it was said to the people long ago, 'You shall not murder, [Exodus 20:13] and anyone who murders will be subject to judgment.'

The NASB version says, "will be subject to the court."

This makes perfect sense, right? Murderers are put on trial and their destiny is "subject" to the jury and the evidence found. But as Jesus does in the Sermon on the Mount, He continues to command us to live at a level much higher and shockingly says the same consequence for murderers is the same as those who… um, get ANGRY?!

22 But I tell you that anyone who is angry with a brother or sister will be subject to judgment.

NOTE: Some manuscripts say, "brother or sister without cause."

That is some serious stuff right there my brother!

Jesus is comparing certain types of anger with MURDER! And both receive the consequence of judgment!

Before you pack your bags and run to a hideout, not all anger is "bad." So, how do we know where we cross the line? After all, Jesus walked into the temple and was furious, flipped over tables, and He lived a perfect life.

Strong's Greek Lexicon

ANGRY

Greek Word: Orgizó (or-gid'-zo)

Definition: to make angry

From the Help's Word-Studies:

Expressing a "fixed anger" (settled opposition).

Are you always angry with your wife? Do you nit-pick at her because of the settled anger in your heart? Are you still punishing her for something a while ago? If so, you are treading on dangerous ground.

"To show settled-opposition") is positive when inspired by God – and always negative when arising from the flesh.

Notice that righteous anger is ok, but it had better be "inspired by God."

Sinful (unnecessary) anger" focuses on punishing the offender rather than the moral content of the offense.

Of course, anything immoral and against the scriptures would qualify as "righteous anger."

EXAMPLE:

If, at dinner, she decides to tell an off-color joke that is inappropriate, this would require correction, but with grace. Let's call it, "Gracefully Corrected." Then drop the issue and do not "punish" her for it.

In this example, you have focused on the moral content of the crude joke/comment and not focused on "making her pay."

But what if, at that same dinner, you catch another male flirting with her? She does not respond to him and makes it clear she is married. Do you get upset with her over that? If so, you are out of order.

That is anger "without cause." It can also be defined as, "unnecessary anger."

The last story is a real-life example! Ridiculous!

Look at the punishment for murder:

Numbers 35:31

"'Do not accept a ransom for the life of a murderer, who deserves to die. They are to be put to death.

Stop killing your wife with unnecessary anger! If you are constantly angry with her, maybe it is not her who needs the heart transplant.

The Godly Strong Rhema Translation

Matthew 5:22

But I tell you that any husband who has fixed and unnecessary anger toward his wife will be subject to judgment.

CHALLENGE QUESTIONS

List some ways you have exhibited fleshly and unjustified anger:

How could you have handled it differently?

Are you still angry about it (fixed anger is wrong regardless if it is justified anger or not)?

If yes, what must you do in order to fully forgive, not allow the devil to scheme you, and move forward?

How can you recognize righteous anger versus sinful anger?

The Godly Strong Challenge

Every time you start to get angry, think about:

- Is this situation worth getting angry over? (Unnecessary anger)
- Is this the type of anger God would approve in this scenario?
- If you were making your wife angry in the same scenario, how would you like her to respond to you? PS: Don't be a hypocrite!
- If you have the right to exhibit "righteous anger," figure out ways to "gracefully correct" your wife instead of overreacting with emotion.

DON'T BE STUPID!

One way to create a false doctrine is to take scripture out of context. The one we are about to explore fits in that category as it is misused about as much as any other scripture between Genesis and Revelation.

To make matters worse, not only is it taught incorrectly, it is often used as a weapon to prevent one from being corrected.

Matthew 7:1

"Do not judge, or you too will be judged."

That has been turned into, "You can't judge me!"

You might use this response in an argument with your wife, or she might even use it on you when a wrong is pointed out. If so, there is a lot to be learned!

But in reality, that response screams, "GUILTY," doesn't it?

Unfortunately for those who use this tactic, scripture calls us to be righteous judges of those who proclaim Christianity.

John 7:24

Do not judge according to appearance, but judge with righteous judgment.

And...

1 Corinthians 5:12

What business is it of mine to judge those outside the church? Are you not to judge those inside?

Therefore, if someone claims to be a believer and says they cannot be judged, they would be W-R-O-N-G.

We also must understand the reason we are to "judge" those who claim to be Christians, and that is twofold:

- To bring correction.
- To bring repentance.

That is the purpose. But if your judgment on someone is to tell them how wrong they are and condemn them, then your judgment is in error.

John 3:17

For God did not send his Son into the world to condemn the world, but to save the world through him.

That leads to this question:

What is your heart behind correcting your wife? To prove how wrong she is and how much better you are? Or, to correct her in a Godly way so change can take place; drawing her closer to Jesus?

By the way: Correction is not griping at her because she put the toilet paper roll "under" and you like it "over."

107

As the spiritual leader of the home, it is sometimes necessary to correct your wife. The heart behind why you do it is critical. Therefore, whenever a scenario arises that requires this type of correction, keep the two principle goals in mind.

Oh, and by the way: If the wife corrects you for something? honor her by listening. You never know; she just might be right. And if so, learning this error in your life gives you the opportunity to grow. That does not happen with a response of, "You can't judge me!" Pride will kill you.

CHALLENGE QUESTIONS

When you "judge" your wife in any way, what should be your motive?

1.

2.

Do you approach her with gentleness and understanding?

___ Yes ___ No ___ Sometimes ___ Rarely ___ Never

How do you react when your wife approaches you with correction?

Do you react to her the same you would like her to react to you?

Do you receive that judgment as correction, or do you cop a 'TUDE?

_____ I receive it willingly

_____ I receive it with resistance.

_____ I do not listen because I already know it all.

_____ I do not listen because it is not her place to correct me (in which case, you would be W-R-O-N-G again!)

The Godly Strong Challenge

Analyze your motives every time you want to correct your wife. What is the purpose behind it?

Additionally, how do you respond when your wife makes an attempt to set you straight in an area she notices could be improved? If the answer is resistance, or "not too well," then work on your mindset to receive correction with humility instead of pride.

Proverbs 12:1

Whoever loves discipline loves knowledge, but he who hates correction is STUPID.

Don't be stupid!

PLANK ALERT!

Context is everything!

The last devotional explained what the motives should be behind correction. The two primary goals are:

- Correction
- Repentance

This devotional runs alongside the last one and is to ensure you do not take a plank upside the head!

Continuing with last week's scripture:

Matthew 7:1-5

1 "Do not judge, or you too will be judged.

2 For in the same way you judge others, you will be judged, and with the measure you use, it will be measured to you.

So, what then, does this scripture really mean? It is pretty simple!

The context is that you are not to "judge" others if you are doing the same thing.

EXAMPLE: You cannot correct a fellow husband for checking out other women when you are checking out other women as well!

That would make you a, well, what is the word? Oh yeah, HYPOCRITE!

Continued…

---

3 "Why do you look at the speck of sawdust in your brother's eye and pay no attention to the plank in your own eye?

4 How can you say to your brother, 'Let me take the speck out of your eye,' when all the time there is a plank in your own eye?

5 You hypocrite, first take the plank out of your own eye, and then you will see clearly to remove the speck from your brother's eye.

In general, most people have a lack of awareness that they do the very same things that annoy and frustrate them when someone else does it. Sometimes, we do not even realize those annoying things are things we do ourselves!

Maybe a husband gets upset because his wife consistently leaves her toothbrush on the sink instead of putting it back in the holder. Yet, after an evening of watching TV, there is a really good chance that the husband's shoes are still in the living room floor.

It can be something as minor as that. Obviously, it can bleed into the bigger things such as money management.

Maybe a wife sees a sale on perfume and purchases a $50 bottle for $30. The husband then gripes at his wife for spending money they "do not have." Two days later, the husband goes golfing with his buddies an spends $75 on green fees alone.

Sometimes we do these things and are completely oblivious. And sometimes we do it and know exactly what we are doing.

It is one thing to be an unaware hypocrite. It is another thing to be a purposeful one.

The Godly Strong Rhema Translation

Matthew 7:3-5

3 "Why do you look at the $30 bottle of perfume on your wife's shelf and pay no attention to the $75 green fee spent to play golf?

4 How can you say to your wife, 'stop buying perfume because we cannot afford it,' all the while there is $75 missing from your bank account?

5 You hypocrite, first stop paying $75 to go play golf, and then you will see clearly to advise your wife to stop buying $30 perfume.'

CHALLENGE QUESTIONS

Are there any issues that have come to you while reading this, or you knew prior, that you are just as guilty as your wife?

_____ Yes _____ No

If so, list them here and write down how you will correct these things in a Godly way.

The Godly Strong Challenge

In everything your wife does this week that annoys you, angers you, rubs you the wrong way, or even something that goes against scripture that you recognize, do a self-analysis and determine whether or not you do the same thing.

If so, get that corrected first before getting upset with your wife.

To make it more fun, let's make a game out of it to keep tensions lower when correction happens.

Have your wife yell out, "PLANK ALERT!" every time you get frustrated with her over something and she recognizes you do the very same thing. This goes both ways, so why not have fun in bringing awareness to each other?

Then, the one with the most "plank alerts" wins and gets to choose their reward! (Within reason, of course!)

LISTEN UP!

Have you ever had a conversation with someone who you could tell was not really listening?

Maybe in the middle of your sentence, their cell phone dings and they immediately glance down at it; missing the rest of what you were saying.

Maybe they interrupt to give their opinion without fully hearing you. They are really saying, "What I have to say is more important than what you are saying." Getting interrupted without being able to finish a sentence is just awesome, right?

Or maybe they just have a look on their face that is telling you, "I really do not care about this."

Have you ever experienced this? Of course, you have.

Have you ever done this to your wife? Of course, you have!

Listen up, fellas! Communication – or a lack thereof - is a common theme when discussing barriers in marriage. Expressing your point is only part of the communication process because listening is also a part of it.

James 1:19

My dear brothers and sisters, take note of this: Everyone should be quick to listen, slow to speak and slow to become angry...

Sometimes, the wife will want to tell you about things of which you have absolutely no interest.

Maybe she wants to tell you about hair products and you shave your head. Maybe she wants to tell you about a new book she is reading. Maybe she wants to tell you about a chick-flick she just watched. How do you respond to those things?

Some of the most common responses are:

- I have no interest in this.
- I am too busy right now.
- I do not care.
- Tell me later.
- I am not in the mood to listen.

What is the theme with the above list? The theme is that all of those excuses are about YOU and not her.

Jesus shows us a great example of how to interact with someone who has something to say.

Matthew 20:29-34

29 As Jesus and his disciples were leaving Jericho, a large crowd followed him.

"Large crowds followed," which means His surroundings in this moment were anything but quiet and peaceful. He also had His buddies hanging with Him, too.

30 Two blind men were sitting by the roadside, and when they heard that Jesus was going by, they shouted, "Lord, Son of David, have mercy on us!"

These men recognized who Jesus was. They knew, from His reputation, how He would respond to them and what He could do for them.

> 31 The crowd rebuked them and told them to be quiet, but they shouted all the louder, "Lord, Son of David, have mercy on us!"

Despite the noise around them, even to the point of being told to SHUT UP, they wanted the attention of Jesus because He was worth the pursuit!

> 32 Jesus stopped and called them. "What do you want me to do for you?" he asked.

Jesus stopped. He did not keep walking; He did not keep texting on His tablet. He did not say, "Wait for commercial!" He did not say, "I don't have time right now." He gave NO excuses.

After He stopped, Jesus asked what He could do for these men.

33 "Lord," they answered, "we want our sight."

Jesus listened.

> 34-A Jesus had compassion on them and touched their eyes.

The compassion of Jesus was the driving force for His response. He knew how to respond because, well, He listened!

Let's simplify! Memorize it, practice it, and apply it!

Jesus was really, really busy.
- You are busy too, right? Yeah, so no excuse.

Jesus was a man worth going to.
- Are you? What would your wife say?

Those in need were desperate to be heard.
- Is your wife begging for your attention? If so, shame on you!

Jesus stopped everything He was doing.
- How often do you simply stop and intently listen to your wife?

Jesus asked what He could do for them.
- Asking questions when your wife talks shows you are interested in what she has to say. Do you do that?

Jesus learned the need because He listened to them.
- What are your wife's needs? Or do you even know?! If your wife is talking, zip it! You cannot learn if your mouth is moving.

Jesus was driven by His compassion and touched them.
- Do you touch her by listening? Do you touch her by putting your hands on her and praying over her when she is struggling? Or, are you so busy, distracted, and uninterested you would not even know what prayer to pray?

Here is the result of Jesus responding in the way He did, and this could be your result, too!

34B: "Immediately they received their sight and followed him."

You see (as they now do), Jesus knew someone He loved was hurting.

These steps lead to healing – much like the eyes of these men - on issues your wife might be dealing with. Do not block the healing process by going in any other direction than what Jesus did.

And if she wants to talk about random topics of which you have no interest... well, you might have NO INTEREST, but you also have NO EXCUSE. This is your wife. Listening and engaging with her with active listening and effective communication is a great way to build emotional intimacy.

Jesus cares about what we care about; even the smallest of things. What is the reason you should not have that same interest in your wife?

The Godly Strong Rhema Translation

James 1:19

Husbands, take note of this: be quick to listen to your wife, be slow to speak so you can understand her intimately, and be slow to become angry.

When your wife wants your attention, what is your response most of the time?

What about when you are "busy?"

_____ On a scale of 1-10, how well do you pay attention to and listen to your wife?

Do you look her right in the eyes when she is speaking?

If the answer above is anything other than, "yes," then what can you do to ensure you are absolutely focused on her?

Percentage wise, how often do you interrupt her?

What can you do to make sure you do not do this?

How does Jesus listen to you when you talk to Him?

Can you say the same when your wife talks to you?

The Godly Strong Challenge

In reality, we should do more listening than talking. Easier said than done! (See what I did there?)

Begin working on staying focused on your wife when she is speaking. During this focus-time, do more listening than talking.

Also, practice what is called, "reflective listening." That means repeating back to her what you heard. That accomplishes a couple of things:

1. She knows you are paying attention.
2. She can clear up anything you misunderstood.

It takes work, but listening is communication, too! She deserves more than your divided attention.

The Godly Strong Challenge #2

In your own words, write down on a piece of paper how you can apply the very steps Jesus did toward your wife.

SUCK IT UP, BIG BOY!

Pet Peeve Alert! Men who get married and then expect his new wife to be his servant.

In this devotional, we are going with the "less is more" principle" as the following scriptures speak for themselves. Simply analyze whether or not this is your attitude toward your wife.

Matthew 20:27

just as the Son of Man did not come to be served, but to serve, and to give his life as a ransom for many.

Jesus loved pleasing the Father in His servanthood to man. As per usual, we are going to learn a little deeper what it means to serve your wife.

Strong's Greek Lexicon

SERVE

Greek Word: Diakoneó (dee-ak-on-eh'-o)

Definition: To serve, minister

From Help's Word-Studies:

"caring for the needs of others as the Lord guides in an active, practical way."

Notice "needs of others;" not "needs of self."

Also, from the Help's Word-Studies:

Diakoneó comes from the word, "diákonos," which means "Actively serve." Literally it means, "Kicking up dust because "on the move."

Let's say you are on the couch watching TV and you hear your wife in the other room washing dishes. Do you jump off the couch so abruptly to go help (serve) that metaphorically, dust is flying because you are on the move? No? Why not?

When you "kick up dust," you can grab the vacuum and then suck it up, big boy!

Philippians 2:7

Rather, he made himself nothing by taking the very nature [or form] of a servant, being made in human likeness.

You may think you are the "stuff," but Jesus was the stuff! Yet, He made Himself "nothing" for His bride. What makes you think you are too good to do so as well?

The Godly Strong Rhema Translation

Matthew 20:28

"Just as the husband did not come to be served, but to serve his wife, and to give his life as a ransom for her."

Philippians 2:7

Rather, the husband made himself nothing by taking the very nature [or form] of a servant, being made in the likeness of Christ.

THAT, my friend, is how you are the "stuff!"

CHALLENGE QUESTIONS

List the ways you actively serve your wife - outside of working - to the point where you are kicking up dust:

What are her needs you are caring for in this servant role?

What other things besides the above could you do to continue serving your wife?

The Godly Strong Challenge

In the upcoming week, focus on serving your wife more than she serves you. That is, it. Oh yeah, and without expectations of something in return. That way, you BOTH win! That is true servanthood!

Then, document how you serve your wife. With each item of servanthood, write down how she responded, and then write down how it made you feel to serve her.

After that, work to be not just a servant, but a consistent one.

Response:

IT'S A TWO-WAY STREET

A husband once told his wife, "I am the head of the house! You obey me!" That is what Ephesians 5 is all about, right?

Let's look at three verses to serve our ego!

Ephesians 5:22-24

22 Wives, submit yourselves to your own husband.

23 For the husband is the head of the wife.

24 Wives should submit to their husbands in everything!

And there you have it! It is right there! But there is a problem; most, including Christians, read the verses just as they are presented above, which is a worldly view. The core intent of presenting scripture in such a way is simple: SELFISHNESS!

This scripture does not give you the authority of dictatorship or, "what you say goes." Instead, it challenges you to live a life as close to Christ as you can.

"But it says the wife is to submit!"

Yeah, but that is the worldly view. Let's check out the verse in full.

Ephesians 5:22

*Wives, submit yourselves to your own husbands
as you do to the Lord.*

Now, it is no longer how the world, and some Christians, view
it.

Strong's Greek Lexicon

SUBMIT

Greek Word: Hupotassó (hoop-ot-as'-so)

The word hupotassó comes from these two Greek words:

Greek Word:	Hypó	Tásso
Definition:	By, Under	To draw up in order, arrange

This is what we get:

*Properly: "Under God's arrangement," i.e., submitting to the
Lord (His plan).*

Additionally, hupotassó is a reflexive verb which means the object
and subject are the same. For the action to take place, someone must
be willing to do it. Example:

"I wash my face." It is a reflexive action the subject willingly does.

A false interpretation would be, "Wash your face, woman!" That is
not a reflexive action!

Another use of this Greek word is, "I submit myself."

That means the wife has a responsibility to "willingly submit" to her husband; not for you to demand her to do it.

The interesting thing about submission is husbands start quoting this scripture because they know it so well. What they do not quote is the verse just before this one, which also uses the same Greek word, "Hupotassó :

Ephesians 5:21

Submit to one another out of reverence for Christ.

NOOOOOO!

That verse begins the segment, "instructions for Christian households." If you do not think this verse is included in those "instructions" and it really starts with verse 22, let's look at how it is written in its original form.

Before reading, understand when the Bible was written, it was not written with verses and chapters. These are letters just like you would send a letter to a friend far away. The verses and chapters were only added later to make it easier to find certain scriptures. With that being said, here is how it was written:

---

*"Submit one to another out of reverence for Christ,
wives to your own husbands as you do to the
Lord..."*

They are connected. That means, dude, that you also have the opportunity to "willingly submit" to your wife.

"But I am the head!"

If you still have that attitude, you should probably rephrase that statement: "But I am the butt-head!" You truly have no clue what being

127

the head of the wife is if this is your mindset. But do not worry! Help is on the way!

By the way: have you ever quoted the following verse in your super-human husband powers?

Colossians 3:19

Husbands, love your wives and do not be harsh with them.

Strong's Greek Lexicon

HARSH

Greek Word: Pikrainó (pik-rah'-ee-no)

Definition: To make bitter

"Husbands, love (agapaó) your wives and do not make them bitter."

Men get laser focused on the beginning of Ephesians 5:22 and forget that it says, "as you do to the Lord." It is an egomaniacal approach grounded in the disease of self-seeking arrogance.

One more nail in the macho coffin.

Unfortunately, Ephesians 5:22 has also been interpreted, "Wives, obey (submit to) your husbands" as if the wife have no say whatsoever.

The implication with this interpretation is that the wife has to obey the husband just as children have to obey parents. Fortunately, we can go to the next chapter for comparison!

Ephesians 6:1

Children, obey your parents in the Lord, for this is right.

It makes sense here that "obey" would mean, "do what is told to you," right? Isn't that the same interpretation just mentioned above about the wife and submission to the husband? Let's find out!

Strong's Greek Lexicon

OBEY

Greek Word: Hupakouó(hoop-ak-oo'-o)

Definition: to listen, attend to

From Help's Word-Studies:

Greek Word:	Hypó	Akoúō
Definition:	Under	Hear

When you put those together, here is what it means:

To obey what is heard (literally, "under hearing").

Additionally:

"Acting under the authority of the one speaking, i.e., really listening to the one giving the charge (order).

"To hearken, obey") *suggests attentively listening, i.e., fully* *compliant (responsive)."*

So, the Greek word in Ephesians 5:21 (22) for "submit" is not the same as "obey" in Ephesians 6:1. "Submit," again, is a reflexive verb meaning, "I willingly submit myself under God's arrangement."

"Obey" in Ephesians 6:1 is not the same. Besides, your wife is not your child.

The Lord does not "force" anyone to submit to Him. His character is one that presents an invitation to willingly submit to Him and His ways because of who He is.

That leads to this question: Does your wife feel oppressed by the way you handle your leadership role?

Oppress means:

"To keep someone in subservience and hardship, especially by the *unjust exercise of authority."*

And what is subservience?

"willingness to obey others unquestioningly."

That would be the faulty interpretation of Ephesians 5:22, that the wife is simply to submit, no questions asked, PERIOD.

If you are using your role as "head of the wife" to make her "obey you unquestioningly," we have a problem. More specifically, YOU have a problem.

Psalm 72:4

May he defend the afflicted among the people and *save the children of the needy; may he* <u>*crush*</u> *the* *oppressor.*

To use your "authority" in this manner is unjust. Being the verse in Psalms says He will "crush the oppressor." Does it make sense for God to crush someone who is doing His will accordingly? Of course not.

considering He will crush those who oppress, that makes it impossible for the word hupotassó to mean, "submit yourself without questioning and do what you are told!"

The condition and motive of your heart is everything!

The Godly Strong Rhema Translation

Ephesians 5:22

Wives, willingly give your husband permission to lead and guide you just as you have given Jesus permission to lead and guide you.

PS: At the beginning it was mentioned some husbands have said, "I am the head of the house! You obey me!" FYI: The Bible does not say the husband is the "head of the house." It says, "head of the wife." It is one of those scriptures that is quoted in error so often that people gloss over it and do not catch the wording.

Technically, the husband and wife both are "heads of the house." Your roles within the house are simply different, but every structure needs a leader that is always looking out for the best interest of those they lead.

Are you operating in a way that is self-serving, wife-serving, or a little of both?

If you had the option to allow someone to lead you that had your character, would you "give them permission" to lead you?

Do you present the same character and opportunity to your wife that Jesus does to you?

_____ On a scale of 1-10, how well do you lead your wife spiritually?

What are your strengths and weaknesses in spiritual leadership?

What can you do to strengthen those weaknesses?

The Godly Strong Challenge

Does your lifestyle present an invitation to your wife to willingly submit to your leadership with confidence? Or does your "leadership" cause her to be bitter?

Be real with yourself and make the necessary adjustments.

Jesus is the type of man the wife can submit to. Are you?

BE AN IDIOS!

We are going to stay with Ephesians 5:22. The reason? It is such a "cliché" verse that we miss the responsibility this verse says the husband has.

"I know, I know. Love my wife as Christ loved the church so she is willing to submit to me. I got it."

Nope. You are an idios. Seriously, not kidding... you are an idios.

Ephesians 5:22

Wives, submit yourselves to your own husbands as you do to the Lord.

Strong's Greek Lexicon

OWN

Greek Word: Idios (id'-ee-os)

Definition: one's own, distinct

You are distinctly your wife's own. But "own" has a little more meaning than you realize.

"Uniquely one's own" is stronger than the simple possessive pronoun ('own'). This emphatic adjective means 'private, personal'" (WS, 222)"

It emphasizes it more than a general meaning. You are her OWN husband! All hers, private and personal; nobody else's, PERIOD!

This is the beauty of marriage when it is done appropriately!

Considering that, what responsibilities does this carry for the husband?

First, you hold the key to this woman's heart. In general, women have an emotional bank account that needs to be filled. There are parts of her that can only be fulfilled by you, and if you do not do it, where does that leave her?

God created us in such a unique way, especially in the bond of marriage.

One person, and one person only, can fill up the emotional areas of a wife, and that is the role of a husband. And before you start making lame excuses, God designed you to be able to do it. If you are not, then get out of your own way and make it happen. God did not accept the excuses of Moses, and He is not going to accept yours.

God also created the wife with physical and sexual needs. Just like the emotional needs, only one man is responsible for taking care of her physically and sexually. That is, you! Unless there are physical and/or health issues that prevent you from being able to be physically intimate with your wife, then what is holding you back?

Notice how we just discussed Genesis 2:24-C (unite to your wife) and Genesis 2:24-D (the two shall become one flesh)?

This means you have to set boundaries around yourself and the things that interfere with you being the husband you are called to be. Why? You are "set apart" for your wife and you have a role to fulfill.

Paul, a servant of Christ Jesus, called to be an apostle and set apart for the gospel of God...

Set apart in Greek means, "to mark off by boundaries from."

Those boundaries are there to protect our relationship with Jesus. If we have the same "boundaries" (or lack thereof) as the world view, then we are not really set apart, are we? Same thing applies to the wife.

No other man can intimately hug her, kiss her, listen to her, support her, encourage her, be her biggest fan, spiritually lead her, pray for her, etc. like you can. You are IT! If you do not provide for her in these areas (remember the word "provide" from earlier?),, then you are robbing her of her blessing, and you of yours.

And oh yeah, you are distinctly her own which means she is distinctly your own as well. So get your eyes off of those other women and honor your wife!

Wives, submit yourselves to your idios husband as you do to the Lord.

You are her idios! Be proud of that, and don't cause her to change the "S" to a "T!"

Be an idios, baby!

The Godly Strong Rhema Translation

Ephesians 5:22

Wives, submit yourselves to the husband who is distinctly yours, and ONLY yours, as you do to the Lord.

CHALLENGE QUESTIONS

Because you are emphatically and distinctly her own, are there any parts of her that are not fulfilled that can only be filled by you?

If so, why are you robbing her?

How will you correct this?

The Godly Strong Challenge

Recognize that whatever you are holding back from your wife, whether it is any type of intimacy, and ear, a laugh, etc. that you make it your mission to not withhold those things from her. You are IT!

Be the spouse for her that you want her to be for you.

Be irreplaceable, dude!

HEAD OVER HEELS

Trivia question: What scripture is in the top five that most men are able to quote, even if they rarely ever read their Bibles?

Ephesians 5:23

For the husband is the head of the wife..."

Just like verse 22, men can use it as a weapon to manipulate the wife and beat her into submission.

I mean, that is what it says, right? Yes, it is, and men around the world have it memorized!

It is a beautiful verse!

Men love it! Men thrive on it! Men quote it with authority! Men demand it! Men bruise their chest when pounding it while quoting it! And men are WRONG and out of order when they use it like that!

It is another one of those scriptures that is quoted out of context. And like the others, it is the worldly view unless you read the entire verse, which men do not seem to quote.

When husbands quote scriptures out of context for personal gain, it is a very dangerous place to tread. To use God's Word and twist it to fit a narrative is dancing with the devil.

Speaking of the devil, let's check out a story where he did the very same thing.

Matthew 4:5-7

5 Then the devil took him to the holy city and had him stand on the highest point of the temple.

6 "If you are the Son of God," he said, "throw yourself down. For it is written: '"He will command his angels concerning you, and they will lift you up in their hands, so that you will not strike your foot against a stone."'

In Matthew 4:6, Satan quoted Psalm 91:11-12 to Jesus. He was preaching the Word just like husbands due to their wives! But there is one problem: Satan quoted the Word and was using it out of context, just like husbands quote Ephesians 5:23 and are also out of context (or completely oblivious as to what it really means)! Quoting scripture out of context results in disorder!

Matthew 4:7 goes on to say:

"Jesus answered him, "It is also written: 'Do not put the Lord your God to the test."'

Jesus responds to Satan by quoting Deuteronomy 6:16.

How can Satan, who has no truth in him (John 8:44) quote scripture and still be lying? For the same reason husbands do it: His motivations are self-centered, manipulative, and all for the gain of himself.

Husbands can quote the first part of Ephesians 5:23 like their social security number if their authority is questioned and things are not falling into place as they wish. It is the "go-to" verse of men who, well, don't really have a clue.

When you quote Ephesians 5:23 with a self-serving goal; putting your wife in the same role as a door mat, it is not going to go well for you. Speaking deceptively about scripture does not change its truth.

Religious abuse, anybody?

It is saddening that there are churches that teach this same concept; as if the wife is not allowed to have a voice. Apparently, those churches also missed Ephesians 5:21, "Submit one to another out of reverence for Christ."

One last thing about quoting this particular scripture:

The men who use it as a manipulation tactic can only quote the beginning. If that is you, here is the verse in its entirety:

Ephesians 5:23

For the husband is the head of the wife as Christ is the head of the church, his body, of which he is the savior.

When you use this verse to get your wife to do what you want out of selfishness, you are contradicting the very nature of Jesus.

The Godly Strong Challenge

Do not use your role as the head to squash her with your heels! Instead, be head over heels about her in a Godly way; valuing her as Christ does the church. He's crazy about us!

The Godly Strong Challenge #2

You have already seen how scriptures can be taken out of context. The Bible says to "study to show yourselves approved (2 Timothy 2:15)." Time to stop riding someone else's coat tails.

SO NOW YOU KNOW!

What is interesting about husbands being the head of the wife is, there is a likely chance most do not know what being the head truly means. We know the general meaning is being a leader, but what is the responsibility that comes along with that title?

You know what a pilot is. But you do not know what all comes along with being a pilot from pre-flight checks to cockpit operation, how to take off, how to land, etc. All you really know is that pilots fly planes unless you are a pilot yourself. All a majority of husbands know is being the head of the wife is being her leader, if they even know that much.

Ephesians 5:23

For the husband is the head of the wife as Christ is the head of the church, his body, of which he is the savior.

Strong's Greek Lexicon

HEAD

Greek Word: Kephalé ((kef-al-ay')

Definition: the head

Shocked?

As mentioned, there are literal and figurative meanings in scripture. In this context, it is impossible for us to be the literal head of the wife. She has her own head! That means we head toward (pun intended!) the metaphoric meaning to bring some clarity. Let's head that way... (UGH)

The Figurative Meaning

A cornerstone, uniting two walls.

So now we have established the husband is the cornerstone (head). What is a cornerstone?

- *A stone that forms the base of a corner of a building, joining two walls.*
- *An important quality or feature on which a particular thing depends or is based.*
- *A rock on which the entire weight of a structure rests.*

Focus on that last definition as we read this next verse.

Isaiah 28:16

So this is what the Sovereign Lord says:

"See, I lay a stone in Zion, a tested stone, a precious cornerstone for a sure foundation; the one who relies on it will never be stricken with panic."

Who is that verse talking about when referring to a "cornerstone?" Jesus! Our entire existence rests on Him as our cornerstone. He is our "sure foundation." If you are truly loving your wife as Christ loves the church, you should be a firm foundation for your wife as well. Are you? Or is your foundation cracked?

141

Using Ephesians 5:23 as a reference, the following diagram is the structure of the marriage covenant. Do not misunderstand it, though. Your wife has every bit as much of direct contact with Christ as you do. However, this diagram (courtesy of Microsoft PowerPoint) is for the marriage covenant only; not for our personal walk with Christ.

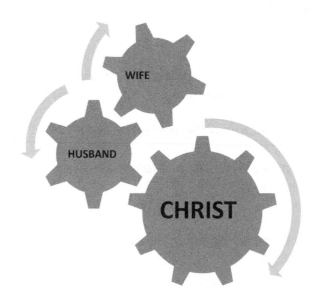

Notice how this works.

If the husband is submitted (connected) to Christ, when the "Christ gear" turns, the husband gear also turns. When the husband gear turns, then the wife gear turns as well, but it starts with Christ.

But what if you are not submitted (connected) to Christ? Not only does your gear not turn, but neither does your wife's gear (in the marriage covenant).

But if all are connected and submitted the way God has laid out, then you are behind one smooth running machine!

Take a close look at that diagram again and notice the accuracy of the Bible with the definition of cornerstone:

"A stone (husband) that forms the base of a corner of a building (marriage), joining two walls (Christ and the wife)."

It does NOT get any cooler than that! But if you are not rock solid, your marriage is on a faulty foundation.

We can also see this diagram laid out here:

---

1 Corinthians 11:3

But I want you to realize that the head of every man is Christ, and the head of the woman is man, and the head of Christ is God.

God is not playing. If you are married, you are the head of your wife. Your lack of desire to fulfill your role in that does not change the purpose. Unfortunately, husbands want the title of "head of the wife," but they do not want the responsibility! But that is not what the scripture mandates.

Luke 12:48

But the one who does not know and does things deserving punishment will be beaten with few blows. From everyone who has been given much, much will be demanded; and from the one who has been entrusted with much, much more will be asked.

So now you know! Being a husband is not just a cool title. You have been given a wife; therefore, much is demanded. You have been entrusted with taking care of her, so much is required!

The Godly Strong Rhema Translation

Ephesians 5:23

For the husband is the cornerstone of the wife; he is the rock of which the entire weight of the marriage structure rests.

How do ya like me now?!

CHALLENGE QUESTIONS

What does being "head of the wife" mean to you now?

How accurate is this scripture in describing you?

- *A tested stone* – have you passed the tests and stood strong for you and your wife?
- *A precious cornerstone* – does your wife see you as precious? Or, would she describe you some other way that is not so glamourous?
- *A sure* foundation – well?
- *The one who relies on it will never be stricken with panic* - Does your wife have THAT type of confidence in you? Why or why not?

The Godly Strong Challenge

Get before Christ and ask Him to reveal ways you can be a better husband and leader.

Pray this scripture over yourself and allow Him to develop you into the Godly Strong husband He has called you to be!

Psalm 139:23-24

23 Search me, God, and know my heart; test me and know my anxious thoughts.

24 See if there is any offensive way in me, and lead me in the way everlasting.

I'M DYING TO LOVE YOU!

Let's say you are a classic car aficionado. You can name all the years, makes, models, all the special features of each, etc.

There is a classic car show at the local fairgrounds you cannot wait to attend. But earlier in the day, a huge storm rolled through the area; BLOWING disgusting elements of nature all over the place!

When you get to the car show, all of the cars sitting outside are covered in mud. This dulls the "shine" on the car, the chrome wheels are covered, but you still see the beauty in the classic car that is your favorite, right? Why is that? Because you know underneath the mess, there is something gorgeous

---

Ephesians 5:25

Husbands, love your wives, just as Christ loved the church and gave himself up for her...

Let's focus on, "Husbands, love your wives, just as Christ loved the church…"

Strong's Greek Lexicon

LOVE

Greek Word: Agapaó (ag-ap-ah'-o)

Earlier, we discussed this word when referring to Romans 5:8 (Agape). Agapaó is the verb form of that word.

Definition: To love.

While that definition seems simple enough, there is so much more to it!

The Strong's Greek Lexicon also adds this:

- *For the believer, preferring to "live through Christ."*
- *embracing God's will (choosing His choices) and obeying them through His power.*
- *Preeminently refers to what God prefers as He "is love."*
- *With the believer, it means <u>actively</u> doing what the Lord prefers, with Him (by His power and direction).*

Do you love your wife in the way God prefers? Do you love her through His power and direction?

To make this simpler: do you love her based on your character or hers?

When we refer back to Romans 5:8, it is a clear example that Christ loved us so much that He sacrificed Himself although we were His enemy. He loved us based on who HE is; not on who WE are!

Husbands sometimes seem to enjoy nit-picking their wives for a lot of things. An inch to the right or left sometimes can get them a tongue lashing because she had the audacity to do something the husband did not like.

Christ laid down His life for the imperfect church. He loved His church through their faults, rebellion, and through every single imperfection they had. That is because He saw through those things and recognized the value each person has to the point He decided they were worth dying for.

Christ died for your wife's imperfection, so stop condemning her because she has them. Oh yeah, He died for yours, too!

He sees past our dirt, He sees past our faults, He sees past our imperfections; yet, we tend to expect more out of our wives than we expect out of ourselves. And when that is not met, we get frustrated. But if we husbands would just look at our wives as Jesus looked at us, which is through spiritual eyes, you would see the preciousness and value in her, even through all of the faults.

Make note of this, though: He lovingly corrects us when we are in error, especially when regarding sinful behavior.

PS: Things like burning dinner do not require correction!

The Godly Strong Rhema Translation

Ephesians 5:25

Husbands, love your wives, just as Christ loved the church and gave himself up for her...

No rhema needed! But a rock solid understanding of the character of Jesus is!

What are some of the faults you see in your wife that you are having a tough time overlooking?

What are some healthy ways you can respond to it/them?

Describe below how you feel Jesus sees your wife.

How do you see her in relation to how you believe Jesus sees her?

What are your takeaways from, "I'm Dying to Love You?"

The Godly Strong Challenge

Ask God to help you see your wife through His eyes; not yours! That's it!

GIVE IT UP!

Continuing with Ephesians 5:25...

Husbands, love your wives, just as Christ loved the church and gave himself up for her.

One thing we learn in this verse is the ultimate way Christ loved His church. And that is, He "gave Himself up for her."

We can come to so many different conclusions about this meaning, and there are certainly a variety of ways to "give ourselves up for our wives."

Strong's Greek Lexicon

GAVE

Greek Word: Paradidómi (par-ad-id'-o-mee)

Definition: to hand over, to give or deliver over, to betray

Wow, that does not sound like much fun, does it?

You cannot be selfish and/or full of pride and be able to "give yourself over" to your wife. This requires complete focus in making sure she is your priority.

Too many times, the wife is the one making the husband priority and the husband decides he will do whatever he wants. This definitely causes issues within the marriage and is not Christ-like at all.

When you said, "I do," you could have also said, "I deliver myself over to you."

This is how you make it a joyful thing for your wife to "submit" to you as Ephesians 5:22 states. When you operate within these characteristics:

- To give oneself up for
- Give oneself to death for
- To undergo death for (the salvation of) one,

That is when your wife sees Jesus in you.

Let's dig a bit deeper into this word and learn from where it comes.

Greek Word:	Pará	Dídōmi
Definition:	Close Beside	Give

So, what does that give us?

"To give (turn) over; "hand over from," i.e. to deliver over with a sense of close (personal) involvement."

Hmm, "close, personal involvement?" You have to love the scriptures! Refer back to "what God has joined together" for the similarities to illuminate themselves right before your very eyes!

Most men say they will die for their wives, and that is a good thing. But the real question is, are you willing to LIVE for her? Christ died, yes. But He also LIVED so that our future could be secure.

151

"Real leadership is leaders recognizing that they serve the people that they lead." -Pete Hoekstra

The Godly Strong Rhema Translation

Ephesians 5:25

Love your wife in the same way Christ loved the church, delivering yourself over for her.

CHALLENGE QUESTIONS

Rate how you do with each of these "in the same way" scriptures:

John 10:10-11

10 The thief comes only to steal and kill and destroy; I have come that they may have life, and have it to the full.

_____ / 10

---

11 I am the good shepherd. The good shepherd lays down his life for the sheep.

_____ / 10

How secure does your wife feel her future is with you because of the way you live for her?

The Godly Strong Challenge

While this is a challenging message, it is possible.

Scripture will not instruct us to do things we are incapable of doing. That is not the way God rolls. He sets us up for success; not failure.

With that, challenge yourself to crucify your flesh and give yourself to your wife more than you ever have. Do this with humility so that she is prioritized and lifted up.

It might not result in an immediate and recognizable way, but inside of her, it will make a difference. Otherwise, we would not have been told to do so.

Besides, love is action; not motivation to get something in return. Rather, it is to glorify God.

THAT'S WHAT I CALL HIGH QUALITY H2O!

Remember that classic car you love so much that was covered in mud after the rainstorm? Washing away all of that muck allowed the beauty of that car to be seen more clearly. How does this apply to marriage and more specifically, you being the spiritual leader of your wife?

Ephesians 5:26

To make her holy, cleansing her by the washing with water through the word.

5:26-A, "To make her holy."

We will not address this in-depth. But it is beneficial to know this also means, "set apart." And exactly how did He set apart His bride?

By applying 26-B.

"... cleansing her by the washing with water through the word."

Let's go through this step-by-step to really grasp what being the spiritual leader requires of you as a husband. Remember, the only way to remove sin is through the blood of Christ. Only He can do that. But as Christians, when we see someone in sin, we are to help correct in a Godly and loving way. But do not try and help your wife in areas of which you are still guilty. PLANK ALERT!

You may have heard this before, but it is worth repeating:

Correction of sin has two goals, and if you do not approach your wife with this motivation, you are approaching it incorrectly.

- Correction
- Repentance

Do you see condemnation on that list? Do you see "to punish" on that list? Do you see "to make them feel guilty" on that list? Of course not. So, keep that in mind as we move through 26-B.

Strong's Greek Lexicon

CLEANSING

Greek Word: Katharizó: (kath-ar-id'-zo)

Definition: To cleanse

Properly: "Without a mixture"; what is separated (purged), hence "clean" (pure) because unmixed (without undesirable elements).

Purged? Where have we heard that?

Figuratively: spiritually clean because purged (purified by God), i.e. free from the contaminating (soiling) influences of sin.

Key words here: "Purified by God (not the husband)." But you can help lead your wife in a way that encourages spiritual growth as the head of the wife! To do that, you have to be a man after God's heart.

Now we head into the part which is the emphasis of Ephesians 5:26. There are not enough bold fonts to capture the importance of what you are about to learn.

"By the washing with water through the word."

To clean that classic car, you have to use water and cleaning materials, right? That is obvious, so we will not dig into the "washing with water." But how do we "wash with water?" It's "through the word."

This is where the scriptures get even more ridiculously awesome!

Remember the two types of words that were discussed in the beginning? The logos word and the rhema word.

The logos word is the general Word of God. And obviously, the rhema word is more specific as you have seen in, "The Godly Strong Rhema Translation" throughout this book.

Before reading further, do you believe the use of "word" in Ephesians 5:26 is logos or rhema? Think about it, and let's find out!

Strong's Greek Lexicon

WORD

Greek Word: Rhema (hray'-mah)

Definition: A word, by implication a matter

"The word rhema comes from rhéō, which means: "to speak") – a spoken word, made "by the living voice" (J. Thayer)."

That gives us: *"The Lord speaking His dynamic, living word in a believer to impart faith ("His inwrought persuasion")."*

So, faith proceeds from (spiritual) hearing; moreover this hearing (is consummated) through a rhēma-word. This is confirmed here:

Romans 10:17

So faith comes from hearing, and hearing from the (rhema) Word of Christ.

Considering the Bible is the logos Word of God, which leads to the rhema Word of Christ, we can draw this powerful conclusion:

You CANNOT lead your wife in the RHEMA word if you are not in the LOGOS word!

He will give you revelations as you are in His word studying, and speak (RHEMA) to you during prayer times that will help you lead your wife (and marriage) in a more "specific" way! Leading your wife in this way will help lead her closer to Jesus. The growth that comes from your leadership is how you assist in the cleansing process!

Teach her the logos word and share with her the rhema word!

The Godly Strong Rhema Translation

Ephesians 5:26

"Setting her apart for a purpose, with you as her spiritual leader, helping her purge undesirable elements by the washing with water through God dynamic and living word spoken to you."

How powerful is THAT? Remember, to do this, you must "give yourself over" as instructed in Ephesians 5:25.

You can "give yourself over" to her first by "giving yourself over" to God and allowing Him to lead you. That way, you know how to lead your wife. Law of order, dude!

Considering a 7-day week, how often are you in the logos word?

_____ / 7

Considering a 7-day week, how often are you in prayer, especially over your wife?

_____ / 7

How well can you lead your wife spiritually with the amount of time you just answered?

How badly do you want to be a stronger spiritual leader?

What is stopping you?

Are the answers you just gave reasons or excuses?

What are you going to do about it?

The Godly Strong Challenge

Regardless of how much you are in God's Word, this challenge is to get you in it more, studying more instead of just reading, and really commit to being the husband you are called to be.

If you are not reading your Bible at all, then start with at least 5-10 minutes per day. Everybody can do that. Then, at least 5 minutes of prayer time.

For those that are already maximizing your time, keep it up!

To help you in this challenge, get a friend (if you haven't already) to hold you accountable in your daily prayer and reading plan. You can return the favor for him, too!

WHAT WOULD YOU LIKE FOR YOUR SIDE?

Imagine you are sitting in your favorite steakhouse. You can smell that luscious aroma coming from the kitchen making your stomach purr like a content cat. Your server asks what you would like to eat, and you order your favorite steak. The server asks, "What would you like for your side?"

Of course, you think of something that compliments the steak whether it be a baked potato, salad, etc. Whatever it is you order, it is a suitable accent for your meal.

Ephesians 5:25-27

25 Husbands, love your wives, just as Christ loved the church and gave himself up for her

26 to make her holy, cleansing her by the washing with water through the word,

27 and to present her to himself as a radiant church, without stain or wrinkle or any other blemish, but holy and blameless.

It has been emphasized the importance of leading your wife in a Godly way, giving yourself up, teaching her by example and the rhema word. Leading by this example can help her grow and strive to be more like Jesus. Can she do this on her own? Absolutely! But this is one of your roles as a husband, so there must be something to this leadership thing! Verse 27 gives us the goal of Godly leadership of the wife.

*27 and to present her to himself as a radiant
church, without stain or wrinkle or any other
blemish, but holy and blameless.*

The incredible result of leading your wife as God has called you to gives you the following:

*"a radiant church (wife), without stain or wrinkle
or any other blemish, but holy and blameless."*

This is where we see everything really begin to develop.

Does the church have any blemishes? This scripture says it does not, but in reality, it DOES! So, what is the point behind this scripture?

When we turn our lives over to Jesus, He no longer sees our imperfections, our blemishes, etc. because we are the "righteousness of God."

2 Corinthians 5:21

*God made him who had no sin to be sin [a sin
offering] for us, so that in him we might become
the righteousness of God.*

We make mistakes, we do stupid stuff, but God corrects and if truly repentant, we ask for forgiveness, change our course, and do our best to not make the same mistakes.

So, when it says the church is being presented "without stain or wrinkle," and "without any blemish," it is because that is the way Christ sees the church and those who are in the "righteousness of God."

Now, apply that to your wife! Catching on to the theme?

"True love is not finding the perfect person. It is seeing the imperfect person perfectly." – Sam Keen

Is that not what Jesus did?

Strong's Greek Lexicon

PRESENT:

Greek Word: Paristémi (par-is'-tay-mee)

This word also comes from two other Greek words:

Greek Word:	Pará	Hístēmi
Definition:	Close beside	To stand

And this is what we have:

"to place beside, to present, stand by, appear."

Here is the expanded definition of the Greek word pará:

- *Close beside*
- *"Introduces someone (something) as very "close beside."*
- *An emphatic "from," means "from close beside" ("alongside").*
- *It stresses nearness (closeness) which is often not conveyed in translation.*
- *Usually adds the overtone, "from close beside" (implying intimate participation) and can be followed by the genitive, dative, or accusative case – each one conveying a distinct nuance.*

What is the theme of presenting your wife? CLOSENESS and INTIMACY! This also lines up perfectly with Genesis 2:24 and Matthew 19:6.

But wait! There's more! Keep in mind, "close beside."

Watch how the New Testament, which was written in Greek, lines up with the Old Testament, which was written mostly in Hebrew.

Genesis 2:21-22

21 So the Lord God caused the man to fall into a deep sleep; and while he was sleeping, he took one of the man's ribs and then closed up the place with flesh.

22 Then the Lord God made a woman from the rib he had taken out of the man, and he brought her to the man.

Could we also say, "God PRESENTED her to Adam?!"

And exactly where is the rib? The SIDE!

This symbolism is so beautiful!

If you are one of those men who walks in front of the wife, STOP IT. Walk BESIDE her!

When she is doing something productive or chasing a dream? Stand BESIDE her!

"The woman was made out of Adam's side. She was not made out of his head to rule over him, nor out of his feet to be trampled upon by him, but out of his side to be equal with him, under his arm to be protected, and near his heart to be loved." - Matthew Henry

If your wife is anywhere but beside you as you walk this life together, then your marriage is OUT! OF! ORDER!

She is your helpmate, one suitable for you as the perfect accent, and that means she belongs nowhere else other than by your side.

The Godly Strong Rhema Translation

Ephesians 5:27

Walk beside your wife as a radiant woman of God; a precious daughter of the King, not focusing on her imperfections, but instead, seeing her as without stain or wrinkle or any other blemish.

DISCLAIMER: "not focusing on her imperfections" does not imply you cannot correct in a Godly way. Christ is always teaching us for our growth. Yet, He still sees us as perfect because the sin debt we owed was paid for and now nailed to the cross. We are debt free.

CHALLENGE QUESTIONS

In what ways are you not walking closely beside your wife whether it be practically or figuratively?

What can you do to change that or enhance what you are already doing? Keyword is CLOSE!

What are your takeaways?

The Godly Strong Challenge

You should have mentioned an area or two where you are not walking alongside your wife whether it be practically or figuratively.

This could be something as simple as you not walking beside her as you approach a restaurant, or metaphorically giving her emotional support during tough times, supporting her as she takes college classes to get her degree, etc.

Maybe you have to up your game in watching kids so she can do her homework, maybe she needs a hug when dealing with tough times, and maybe she needs her hand held as you take a stroll.

The challenge is to get laser focused in walking beside her in **P**artnership, **U**nity, and being **T**eammates!

BONUS: The Yoke

This is a great time to share a small bit about the yoke, considering Jesus said we are "yoked together in marriage.".

A yoke usually represented work. The yoke was custom made to fit the shoulders and necks of the animals so that it would not cause pain.

When two animals were yoked together, they had to work in unity to accomplish a common goal.

One experienced ox that was stronger and more trained would be joined – side-by-side - with a less experienced, weaker ox so it could be train as well. That way, that ox could train others in the future.

Sounds a little bit like marriage, doesn't it?

Now we know why Jesus used that specific Greek word when He mentioned, "What God has joined together, let no one separate."

You are to be "side-by-side" with your wife, being joined to her for one purpose, and doing life together. If there is pain in your marriage, someone is tugging against that yoke considering it is custom built to alleviate – or at least minimize – that pain. That means someone is Not working in unison with the other. Is that your marriage? Are you tugging against the marriage yoke?

MY EZER!

In the following questions, what is the first answer that comes to mind?

Who is more important?

In a church: The custodian or the pastor?

In a concert: The musicians or sound engineer?

In the police department: The dispatcher or police officers?

You see, we get this preconceived idea that particular responsibilities and/or roles are more important than another because of how we view them. But as the previous devotional explained, the head cannot tell the foot, "I don't need you!"

Without a clean church, you are more than likely not going to get new attendees, regardless of how well the pastor preaches and teaches.

Without the sound engineer, the band will sound terrible regardless of how talented the musicians are.

The police officer will not know what location to go to without the dispatcher.

This is what we call Partnership, Unity, and teamwork!

According to Oxford Languages, the definition of devaluing is "to reduce or underestimate the worth or importance of."

Devaluing the importance of the custodian, sound engineer, or the dispatcher completely misses the mark. In the same way, devaluing the importance of your wife is treading on dangerous ground. Hopefully, by now being you have reached this point in the book, you are not thinking in this way. But this will help you get even more focused on her value.

We will now dissect the "law of first mention" as it pertains to your wife and her role.

Genesis 2:18

The Lord God said, "It is not good for the man to be alone. I will make a helper suitable for him."

There are two "laws of first mention" in this verse:

1. First mention of something that is "not good," and that is for "man to be alone."
2. The first mention of the role of a wife, and that is a "helpmate."

What does it really say when God says, "It is not good for man to be alone?" It is a two-fold answer.

It is saying if you were so perfect, you would not need a helper! But God recognized you cannot do it on your own. God is perfect and all-knowing. He has the best answers for us in our times of need. He, being an awesome provider, saw the husband needed help, so His "perfect provision" was creating a "helper suitable for him," and the WIFE was created! That, in itself, screams "VALUABLE!"

If you enjoy messing with your friends, go ask them this question:

"Is alone bad? Why or why not?" You are going to get all kinds of answers. But the simple answer is, "Yes." But why?

Strong's Hebrew Lexicon

ALONE

Hebrew Word: Bad - not joking!

Genesis 2:18

"It is not good for man to be BAD."

Ok, back to being serious!

Definition for alone: Separation, apart

Matthew 19:6

"What God has joined together, let no man separate!"

Genesis 2:18

"It is not good for man to be separated (it's BAD!)."

Well, look at that. The Old Testament and New Testament lining right up with each other! But it only gets better!

Strong's Hebrew Lexicon

HELPER

Hebrew Word: Ezer (ay'-zer)

Definition: A help, helper.

Does not look like too big of a deal, does it? Cool. Buckle your seatbelt.

Psalm 118:7A

The Lord is with me; he is my helper.

Let's add that Hebrew word:

The Lord is with me; he is my EZER.

How valuable is she NOW?!

Without God's help, we can do absolutely nothing. But with an ezer, we are powerful together.

At this point, you should have no issue recognizing her value unless you are stubborn (witchcraft), spiritually blind, arrogant (God opposes the proud... James 4:6), or obstinate; unwilling to be persuaded by God's "inworking of faith."

Finally, you read where the "husband is the head of the wife as Christ is head of the church." But we know the husband is NOT Jesus.

Now we read where the wife is our ezer as God is our ezer. But we know your wife is not God.

Isn't it interesting to you that some of the characteristics of God and Jesus were used in the marriage analogy for roles of husband and wife? With that in mind, what does that look like when we operate in a Godly way?

John 14:9

Jesus was talking and said, "Any one who has seen me has seen the Father."

That is because God and Jesus are ONE UNIT but operating in distinct roles. How does that happen?

CLOSENESS, unity, and knowing each other inside and out! Put the word, "know," in your back pocket for later!

With that being understood, this is a helper that is "suitable" for you. What does suitable mean?

From Brown-Driver-Briggs, suitable means in this context:

"A help corresponding to him i.e. equal and adequate to himself."

Again, another way to drive home that she is your equal, not your doormat.

The Godly Strong Rhema Translation

The Lord God said, "It is not good for you to be alone. I will make a doormat suitable for you."

Wait? It does not say that? Of course not!

The Godly Strong Rhema Translation

The Lord God said, "It is not good for you to be separated. I will make {your wife's name} your ezer, who is equal and adequate to you."

List below the specific things your wife does with little or no help from you. (Such as specific household chores, cooking, additional income, etc.)

What things did you write down that you have never truly appreciated her for doing (yes, this is similar to the gratitude devotional, but it is always good to remember how valuable your wife is!)?

Of the things you listed, which of them would be something you would HATE to do on your own if you did not have your ezer?

Your Godly Strong Takeaways:

The Godly Strong Challenge

Big challenge ahead!

Sit down and write out every single thing of value your wife brings to you and your family as an ezer. This can be things anywhere from doing laundry to being a supportive wife while you chase a dream. Break them down into three categories:

- Spiritual
- Emotional
- Physical/Practical

Then, take this list and put it in a location you will see frequently to keep you focused on her beauty instead of her imperfections if you struggle with that.

GET NAKED!

Was your first thought, "Oh yeah, baby!"? If so, you might be labeled as a "typical man" because, "all men do is think about sex!" Sometimes, that is certainly the only thing on a man's mind, and that is unfortunate because there is so much more to sex than just the physical act. However, God created us as sexual beings, so there is nothing wrong with sex being on your mind (in the marriage covenant) providing there is more to you than that, but we will get to that later. Back to the point.

We learned about "closely walking beside" your wife in different ways, so This will provide a bit of a glimpse as to how to do that on another level. Here is how:

You have to "get naked," but in a way that may be uncomfortable for you. To grow, you must step out of your comfort zone.

If you are uncomfortable with this type of nakedness and think it is too cold, then grab a blanket, grab your wife, and snuggle up with her!

Genesis 2:25

Adam and his wife were both naked, and they felt no shame.

Eve had just been created for Adam and they BOTH were naked. Every part of Adam was accessible to Eve, and every part of Eve was accessible to Adam.

There were no issues with vulnerability; there was nothing hidden from the other; there was transparency there with no limitations, and through all of that, there was no shame! That, my friend, is what marriage is supposed to be!

In general, men are not emotional with their wives. Psychologically, society has taught men if they are vulnerable and show emotions, or are open with their wives, or even if they cry, they are weak. Only someone weak would say that because it takes strength to show this type of vulnerability. Take the topic of crying as an example. Do you think that makes you weak? Does that cause you to feel shameful? Then look at this:

John 11:35

Jesus wept.

The greatest man of all-time was emotional, compassionate, and had no issues shedding tears with and for those He loved. What do you think about crying and being emotional now?!

Men really need to learn how to be vulnerable in front of their wives, telling them what they mean to them, how she blesses you, how she is appreciated, and how you are thankful she is part of your one "physical and marriage" body.

This is difficult for a lot of men, but are you more concerned about how it makes you feel uncomfortable? Or are you more concerned about how it would make your wife feel should you be willing to open up to her, unashamedly, giving every bit of yourself to her? If you would put the macho madness down and be a real man, your wife would likely look at your nakedness in a very, very positive way… if you know what I mean! Give it a shot!

However, this is not about sex but being emotionally connected to your wife. This is part of the pursuit and a way to "keep her close" as explained in Genesis 2:24.

WARNING! When you do, watch the emotional intimacy begin to explode! And oh, no fig leaves needed!

The Godly Strong Rhema Translation

You and your wife should be emotionally and physically naked and feel no shame being vulnerable with each other in either of those ways!

CHALLENGE QUESTIONS

Write down below the things that are very difficult for you to share with your wife on an emotional, vulnerable level.

What is the reason this is hard to share for you?

How can you overcome these things?

What would it do for your wife to open up to her more than ever and let her have the whole of you?

The Godly Strong Challenge

Keep the list handy that you wrote down. This week, start sharing them with your wife one at a time and ask her to help you overcome the hinderances that prevent you from being completely vulnerable and naked with her.

NICE BODY!

Do you work out? If not, do you, um, eat? Do you get up in the morning and brush your teeth? (If not, EWW!) Do you shower and try to look presentable when at work or on a date night with the wife? (If you have not dated her in a while, get on it!) What is the reason you do all of that? It is because you are taking care of yourself, right?

Ephesians 5:28-31

28 In this same way, husbands ought to love their wives as their own bodies. He who loves his wife loves himself.

So, can you love yourself if you do not love your wife? Hmmm…

29 After all, no one ever hated their own body, but they feed and care for their body, just as Christ does the church—

30 for we are members of his body.

31 "For this reason a man will leave his father and mother and be united to his wife, and the two will become one flesh."

We are told we are part of Christ's body; therefore, He "feeds us and cares for us," because He does not hate "His own body."

You and your wife are one marriage body, PERIOD. You, Mr. Corner Stone of the marriage, MUST "feed and take care of it."

It is also important to recognize there are no parts of the body that are of "lesser significance." We have addressed this; however, it seems to be a difficult concept to grasp for a lot of men.

Your pinky seems insignificant… until you no longer have it.

Your little toe seems insignificant… until you no longer have it…

Your wife might seem insignificant to you…. My friend, let's NOT let it get to that point where you might find out! God's way is the ONLY way and is full proof!

Ephesians 4:16

16 From him the whole body, joined and held together by every supporting ligament, grows, and builds itself up in love, as each part does its work.

"As each part does its work." Do your job as husband, and that will help your wife be the helpmate she is called to be.

Keeping in mind you are the head of the wife, let's talk about what happens to the body (wife) if the head (the husband) does not fulfill his purpose.

Imagine someone who may have some sort of brain damage. Does the body function fully? Of course not.

What happened when David drilled Goliath right between the eyes? His entire body collapsed.

What was that? Oh, so you do not think you need your wife. Let's see about that.

1 Corinthians 12:21-26

21 The eye cannot say to the hand, "I don't need you!" And the head cannot say to the feet, "I don't need you!"

Are you one of those who walks around with that chest puffed out, with an ego that you are just so much better than your wife? You are the strong one and she is just so weak? Your incredible machoness makes her look even weaker because, well, "You are the MAN!" Uh-huh… Hoping that is not the case, let's quickly shoot that down.

22 On the contrary, those parts of the body that seem to be weaker are indispensable,

23 and the parts that we think are less honorable we treat with special honor. And the parts that are unpresentable are treated with special modesty,

24 while our presentable parts need no special treatment. But God has put the body together, giving greater honor to the parts that lacked it,

25 so that there should be no division in the body, but that its parts should have equal concern for each other.

26 If one part suffers, every part suffers with it; if one part is honored, every part rejoices with it.

In marriage, there is no such thing as the husband "winning" and the wife "losing." You either win together, or you lose together.

You are one flesh! If you break your ankle, the whole body suffers! If you are a broken husband outside of God's will, your wife also suffers the consequence! Let's reiterate:

25 so that there should be no division in the body, but that its parts should have equal concern for each other.

No division in the body? Genesis 2:24, Matthew 19:6, Genesis 2:18 any one?

Let's tie this together:

Ephesians 5:31-32

31 "For this reason a man will leave his father and mother and be united to his wife, and the two will become one flesh." [sound familiar?!]

32 This is a profound mystery—but I am talking about Christ and the church.

And there you have it. The reflection marriage gives should resemble Christ's relationship with the church (His body).

Closeness and unity are NOT an option when it comes to your marriage fulfilling the purpose God has for it. Is your behavior toward your wife one that enhances God's Kingdom as people see it? Or is it hurting the case for Christ with His relationship with His people?

Just like when God says, "You are either for me or against me," the same principle can be said for marriage. Only half-doing marriage is not doing it at all. You cannot have your "cake and eat it, too."

The marriage covenant is a prized union to God. To deal with your wife treacherously – God's precious daughter - does not fly with Him. When you think of how you treat her, the world views it as how Christ treats the church.

Malachi 2:13-15

13 Another thing you do: You flood the Lord's altar with tears. You weep and wail because he no longer looks with favor on your offerings or accepts them with pleasure from your hands.

14 You ask, "Why?" It is because the Lord is the witness between you and the wife of your youth. You have been unfaithful to her, though she is your partner, the wife of your marriage covenant.

15 Has not the one God made you? You belong to him in body and spirit. And what does the one God seek? Godly offspring. So be on your guard, and do not be unfaithful to the wife of your youth.

16 "The man who hates and divorces his wife," says the Lord, the God of Israel, "does violence to the one he should protect," says the Lord Almighty. So be on your guard, and do not be unfaithful.

Notice:

- God is the witness of your…
- Marriage <u>covenant</u>
- Mentioned body and spirit
- Being unfaithful is mentioned more than once
- You should be protecting your wife

The Godly Strong Rhema Translation

Ephesians 4:16

From the husband the whole marriage body, joined and held together by the husband and wife, grows, and builds itself up in LOVE, as the husband and wife fulfill their God-given role.

List your strong traits in any area(s).

List your wife's strong traits.

List your weaker traits.

List your wife's weaker traits.

How can you two work together better in accenting each other?

Your Godly Strong takeaways:

The Godly Strong Challenge

Read each of these characteristics of why God says He will rebuke your sacrifices and offerings to Him. As you do, think about ways you may be operating in this way... and get it corrected!

The Godly Strong Rhema Translation

Malachi 2:14

You ask, "Why?" It is because the Lord is the witness between you and the wife of your youth. You have been dealing _____ with/against her, though she is your partner, the wife of your marriage covenant.

The word "treacherously is what fills the blank above. The following bullet points are the expanded definitions from the Strong's Hebrew Lexicon of that word.

Read the verse, insert the following words and definitions, then analyze whether or not the verse would accurately describe you.

- *Deceitfully (action or practice of deceiving by concealing or misrepresenting the truth)*
- *Treacherously (guilty of or involving betrayal or deception)*
- *Unfaithfully (covenant unfaithfulness; Hebrews 13:4)*
- *Offending (causing to feel upset, annoyed, or resentful)*
- *Transgressing (going outside the boundaries of scriptural guidelines of a Godly husband)*
- *Departing physically or emotionally (Matthew 19:6;*
- *Genesis 2:24)*

There should not be a HINT of this type of behavior toward your wife (body). If there is, ask God for direction and growth in these areas so you can be even more Godly Strong!

CAN YOU HEAR ME NOW?!

Heading home from work on a bright, sunny day, you are excited to use your brand-new cell phone with your brand-new service to give your wife a call. She answers and you have a question for her.

"Honey, do you want me to pick up some food on the way home?" Her response was, "u ca, ut I wa eady ing ner. But I ill be hap to ut it the frig tor and sa it or rrow."

What in the world did she just say?!

After multiple attempts, you finally get frustrated and hang up. What could be the problem with this brand-new phone and service?

The answer: Your new cell service has no towers in the area where you were traveling and was barely picking up a signal. Because of that, you were hindered from hearing everything your wife had to say. Because you had no experience with the new service, you did not understand that was a bad area with no towers. But with experience of using this service, that is something you would have come to know.

Sometimes, that is the way we feel about God, right? "It is like I am praying, but God does not hear me."

It might be that the answer from God is simply, "No." But there are other reasons that God might not be listening to you such as the following:

185

1 Peter 3:7

*You husbands in the same way, live with your
wives in an understanding way, as with someone
weaker, since she is a woman; and show her
honor as a fellow heir of the grace of life, so that
your prayers will not be hindered.*

To ensure you do not misinterpret this verse, we are going to break it down. Surprised?

---

*"You husbands in the same way, live with your
wives in an understanding way..."*

Understand my wife? Are you kidding me?! But men cannot understand women!

Maybe not, but there is a process to doing your best to understand your wife the best you can.

Strong's Greek Lexicon

UNDERSTANDING

Greek Word: Gnósis: (gno'-sis)

Definition: a knowing, knowledge

From Help's Word-Studies:

This word is derived from ginóskó, which means: "experientially know"

"Working") knowledge gleaned from first-hand (personal) experience, connecting theory to application; "application-knowledge," gained in (by) a direct relationship.

Back to Gnósis:

"Applied knowledge") is only as accurate (reliable) as the relationship it derives from.

The only way you can "apply knowledge" and get it as accurate as possible is to be super close to your wife! If you are not on the same page, not working together, not glued together, it is much more difficult to "understand" her because, "understanding is only as accurate as the relationship it derives from."

If you are distant, you are only going to have a distant understanding of your wife. So, what is the key to understanding her? Walking closely beside her!

You should underline that because it is doubtful you have ever heard anything similar (sarcasm!). You also might want to put the "experientially know" phrase in your back pocket as well!

How about we quickly check out another way to not understand the wife:

Proverbs 18:13

To answer before listening— that is folly and shame.

It is exceedingly difficult to understand someone if you are talking over them. It also is difficult when that phone with bad cell service has your attention instead of her.

Do you look at your phone while she is talking to you? STOP! Put the thing down!

Here is another way to ensure you are unable to understand her better:

Proverbs 15:1

A gentle answer turns away wrath, but a harsh word stirs up anger.

Harsh words... those will make her bitter! (Colossians 3:19)

"As with someone weaker, since she is a woman..."

People get stuck on the "weaker" part of this verse to the point they miss the rest.

When Paul wrote this command to husbands, it was not meant as an insult or a way to degrade women. Frankly, it was quite the opposite. It was an admonition to be considerate of them and understand them. Many women in those days were at a social disadvantage from what we know today.

Everybody struggles to understand the status of someone else; even those we live with. This is why Paul commands husbands to "understand" the wife, and sometimes, that is not an easy task, is it?

Another option could simply mean "physically weaker."

We all know that women in general are "physically weaker" than men, but in context, this does not seem to fit this particular narrative. So, we will go with the former explanation that the wife was not as advantaged in society.

"And show her honor..."

Strong's Greek Lexicon

HONOR

Greek Word: Timé (tee-may')

Definition: a valuing, a price

Wait! Does that also sound familiar to you? If not, this should start ringing the bell!

The word comes from tiō, "accord honor, pay respect").

Properly: Perceived value; worth (literally, "price") especially as perceived honor – i.e. what has value in the eyes of the beholder.

Figuratively: The value (weight, honor) willingly assigned to something.

In the same family of words we find, TIMIOS.

Hebrews 13:4

Marriage is to be held in honor (timios) among all...

You are to assign honor and value to your wife. It is just that simple.

"As a fellow heir of the grace of life…"

Strong's Greek Lexicon

FELLOW HEIR

Greek Word: Sugkléronomos (soong-klay-ron-om'-os)

Definition: a co-inheritor

Usage: a joint heir, participant.

She is part of God's family, too!

Now to the result of dishonoring, having a lack of understanding, and not seeing her as your equal by not respecting or valuing her…

"So that your prayers will not be hindered."

Strong's Greek Lexicon

HINDERED

Greek Word: Egkoptó (eng-kop'-to)

Definition: to cut into, impede, detain

This Greek word is derived from the following:

Greek Word:	En	Kópto
Definition:	In	Cut

190

We get:

Cut into (like blocking off a road); hinder (A-S) by "introducing an obstacle that stands sharply in the way of a moving object" (Souter)

Figuratively: Sharply impede, by cutting off what is desired or needed; to block (hinder).

Are there times you do not feel God hears you? Could this be one of the reasons?

Learn to understand your wife and her value! No, there is no such book entitled, "How to Understand a Wife," so you have to work at it!

The Godly Strong Rhema Translation

1 Peter 3:7

Husbands, in the same way, study your wife and use that first-hand experiential knowledge to understand her better.

Although she is weaker, show her honor by valuing her as a fellow participant in the grace of life so that your prayers will not be Sharply impeded and cut off. Otherwise, God just may not hear what you have to say!

Considering our prayers can be hindered if we do not live with our wives in an understanding and respectful way, how hindered do you feel your prayers might be right now?

How often do you interrupt her when in normal conversations, or especially during conflict?

What tone do you use toward your wife when you respond when things are going well? When things are tense? Are you gentle? Harsh? Understanding?

What kind of experiences can you initiate or draw from to understand your wife better?

Your takeaways from, "Can you hear me now!?"

The Godly Strong Challenge

Figure out ways to understand your wife on a more intimate level. It may simply be to put down your phone while she talks, learning to listen better without interrupting, asking questions about her day, or even learning the things that can frustrate her that she does not talk about, or the things that make her happy that you can continue doing or learn to do.

So many ways to get this knowledge, but it is not going to happen without effort.

The Godly Strong Bonus Challenge

In case you still have a weak signal, here was her response:

"You can, but I have already been cooking dinner. But I will be happy to put it in the refrigerator and save it for tomorrow."

Your bonus challenge? Call her on the way home from work and ask her what she wants for dinner because you are bringing it home.

FOLLOW THE LEADER

It has been said, "leaders lead in a way that those who are following feel as if they are being served."

We husbands have a tough time thinking of our leadership role as one that is meant to serve or submit , especially when it comes to the wife, right?! Right! We have already mentioned we are to lead by example, so if we do not submit in a Godly way, then how will the wife know how to do so?

Submission has become a four-letter word in today's culture, but Godly submission will initiate the Spirit of God in ways that might surprise you.

You have already read where Jesus submitted to the Father's will. He set His feelings aside because He was on a mission. He did not get distracted; He did not let peer pressure sway Him; He did not let the mockers deter Him; He did not let selfishness get in the way; He did not let pride stop Him. Instead, what drove Him was what the Father wanted, and, in turn, what blessed His people.

Matthew 3:13-17

13 Then Jesus came from Galilee to the Jordan to be baptized by John.

This trip was between 60-70 miles... and He walked it. Jesus was on a mission! And you won't even walk to the kitchen to get your wife a drink?

14 But John tried to deter him, saying, "I need to be baptized by you, and do you come to me?"

15 Jesus replied, "Let it be so now; it is proper for us to do this to fulfill all righteousness." Then John consented.

Let's take a quick look at what righteousness is to get a better understanding at what His purpose was in this:

Strong's Greek Lexicon

RIGHTEOUSNESS

Greek Word: Dikaiosuné (dik-ah-yos-oo'-nay)

Definition: Divine approval, or what is approved by God.

Jesus is the head of the church; you are head of the wife. Why is it Jesus can submit to John the Baptist, to fulfill righteousness, because it is "proper," and you struggle with Godly submission to your wife?

Could that be an ego problem?

Now, watch what happens with Godly submission when done appropriately.

16 As soon as Jesus was baptized, he went up out of the water. At that moment heaven was opened, and he saw the Spirit of God descending like a dove and alighting on him.

Did you catch that? Jesus submitted to what the Father wanted, even submitted Himself to John the Baptist, and all that happened was... the Heavens opened, and God's Spirit reigned down!

What did God think of this?

17 And a voice from heaven said, "This is my Son, whom I love; with him I am well pleased."

What an incredible statement by God after the baptism of Jesus. Christ certainly got that "divine approval."

Humbleness starts in the heart, so to get Heaven to open, the Spirit to fall, and obtain that divine approval, you cannot have a haughty, selfish, or dominating attitude.

James 4:6

"God opposes the proud, but gives grace to the humble."

The King of all Kings allowed John to baptize Him as a beautiful example of hupotasso submission; a willingness to submit to God's arrangement.

You see, Godly submission to your wife equals Godly submission to Jesus, and then the Heavens open! This is also a form of worship. How? Read the second half of the verse:

Ephesians 5:21

Submit one to another out of reverence for Christ.

A little more detail:

- Reverenced: "Deep respect for someone or something."
- Worship: "The feeling or expression of reverence; admiration for God"

CHALLENGE QUESTIONS

In Matthew 3:13-17, who was the one submitting in this scenario?

What type of personality traits were needed for this submission?

Do you exhibit those?

What happened after the submission?

Is the way you treat your wife stamped with God's divine approval? Why or why not?

Your Godly Strong takeaways:

The Godly Strong Challenge

The purpose of Jesus was obvious. He wanted to "fulfill all righteousness," and that required focus, investment, intent, and a willingness to fall under God's arrangement and plan.

Examine your marriage this week and look for ways your marriage may not be "under God's arrangement." You can ask your wife to join you in this analysis, or you can do it on your own and then take it to your wife. You can also begin working toward that on your own and pay attention to your wife to see if she notices.

Put those things that are out of order IN order and watch out for God's Spirit to descend like a dove on you and your wife!

The Godly Strong Challenge #2

Just like Jesus submitted to God the Father by submitting to John the Baptist, find ways in the next seven days to submit to your wife in areas where you normally do not. Uncomfortable? Yes. But you cannot grow when you are entrenched in your comfort zone.

You have to start with the small things first to prepare yourself for the bigger things. These types of things will be stamped with God's "divine approval"

You want to eat at your favorite restaurant, and she wants to eat at hers? Go to hers.

She wants to watch her favorite TV show that you do not like? Watch it with her.

She wants you to play a board game and you do not like playing? Play it!

Ask her what she wants to do and bless her with a thankful and joyous heart. "Feelings, whoa, whoa, whoa feelings!" Sacrificial love, dude! Selfishness must die!

YADA, YADA, YADA!

Speaking of ways to worship, how about sex? What?!

There is something fascinating in the scriptures that needs to be revealed. It shows just how intimate this incredible gift from God is in the marriage bedroom. It also reveals the level of intimacy God wants to have with us. If you never have thought of sex with your wife as anything more than a physical act, then I hope this helps you realize it is much, much mor than that.

It is about selflessness, sacrificial love, displaying love toward your wife in the most intimate way possible, and dare we say a form of worshipping God?

It is now time to reveal something really cool…

Jeremiah 31:34

No longer will they teach their neighbor, or say to one another, 'Know the Lord,' because they will all know me, from the least of them to the greatest," declares the Lord. "For I will forgive their wickedness and will remember their sins no more."

In this verse, it is easy to conclude the nature of how intimate God wants to be with His people. They would know God in such an intimate way that He would "forgive their wickedness and remember their sins no more."

Let's check out another scripture.

Exodus 33:13

If you are pleased with me, teach me your ways so I may know you and continue to find favor with you...

Notice the theme of the two scriptures... God desiring to know His people, as well as His people desiring to know Him.

Strong's Hebrew Lexicon

KNOW

Hebrew Word: Yada ((yaw-dah')

Definition: To know

Let's take a left turn.

Genesis 4:1

1 Adam made love to his wife, Eve....

Other translations:

"Now Adam knew his wife Eve..." (ESV)

"Now the man had relations with his wife Eve..." (NASB)

"Relations" is a great translation because you cannot have sex the way God created it without relationship! Otherwise, it is just another act.

You can also find this word in verse 17:

"Cain had relations with his wife..."

Other verses if you care to look them up:

Genesis 2:25, 24:16, 1 Samuel 1:19, 1 Kings 1:4.

Now, check it out!

Strong's Hebrew Lexicon

RELATIONS; KNEW; MADE LOVE

Hebrew Word: Yada ((yaw-dah')

Definition: To know

What a special place the marriage bedroom is supposed to be! Just like God wants to know us intimately, He created a different type of intimacy for the husband and wife to "get to know" each other; with passion, too!

We are to have a level of (spiritual) intimacy with God, and that level of intimacy with Him should not compare with any other. It is Him, and Him ONLY!

Likewise, God calls us to have (physical and sexual) intimacy with the wife, and that level (and type!) of intimacy with her ONLY!

Catching the parallels?

Let's head to the New Testament.

John 10:14

"I am the good shepherd; I know my sheep and my sheep know me..."

Strong's Greek Lexicon

KNOW

Greek Word: Ginóskó (ghin-oce'-ko)

Definition: to come to know, recognize, perceive

From Help's Word-Studies:

Properly: To know, especially through personal experience (first-hand acquaintance).

Yep, firsthand experience! You must invest in your wife to know her emotionally, physically, and sexually.

Does that also sound familiar, by chance? Living with your wife in an understanding way (because of experiential knowledge) so that your prayers are not hindered?

Matthew 1:25

25 But he did not consummate their marriage until she gave birth to a son. And he gave him the name Jesus.

"And Mary [a virgin] said to the angel, 'How will this be since I do not know (ginóskó) a man?'"

It is time to view your sex life with your wife as more than just sex. It is way, way more than that! It is a way to honor God, honor your wife; ensuring her interests and desires are met through sacrificial love, and again, having fun while doing it!

Proverbs 5:18-19

18 May your fountain be blessed, and may you rejoice in the wife of your youth.

19 A loving doe, a graceful deer— may her breasts satisfy you always, may you ever be intoxicated with her love.

In other words: "Yada, Yada, Yada!"

The Godly Strong Challenge

If you have only thought of sex as a physical act, begin renewing your mindset of this new way of thinking; that sex is a gift to be enjoyed by each of you, but should be such an intimate, passionate act that is only shared with each other.

God wants all of you in a different type of intimate way, and you and your wife should want all of each other in THIS unique, distinct, and awesome intimate way!

And have fun with it! In public just say, "Yada, yada, yada!" It is a safe way to flirt without getting caught before getting home to yada!

DO I KNOW YOU?

Earlier, we explored a couple of scriptures that has sexual references:

Hebrews 13:4

Marriage is to be held in honor among all, and the marriage bed (euphemism for sex within the confines of marriage) is to be undefiled; for God will judge the sexually immoral and adulterers.

Then this verse:

"therefore a man shall leave his father and mother and unite to his wife, and the two will become one flesh." (Genesis 2:24, Matthew 19:5, Ephesians 5:31)

Those are vague references of sexual unity that God wants us to have in our marriage. But there is also a scripture putting stipulations on the sexual relationship we are to follow. Unfortunately, this is also a scripture that is often taken out of context.

The unfortunate consequence of misinterpreting scripture, other than you missing what God is truly saying, is that the scripture is more beautiful when it is understood in the way it is meant to be presented.

1 Corinthians 7:2-5

2 But since sexual immorality is occurring, each man should have sexual relations with his own wife, and each woman with her own husband.

This is a given. Anything of a sexual nature that is not 100% meant for your wife is sexual immorality (porneia) such as flirting, porn, fantasizing about other women (and the list goes on), is defiling the marriage bed and adultery. No further explanation needed. If you are trying to justify "window shopping," just stop it. You are wrong. 100% wife; NO other "influences!"

3 The husband should fulfill his marital duty to his wife, and likewise the wife to her husband.

4 The wife does not have authority over her own body but yields it to her husband. In the same way, the husband does not have authority over his own body but yields it to his wife.

Here is where we run into potential problems.

it is common for a husband to be very stern with the wife in quoting this scripture and might say, "You cannot turn me down! The Bible says you have to have sex with me!"

Is that what it really says? Yes, but NO!

It is clear when a man approaches his wife with this attitude, he is thinking more about himself than his wife. With that type of attitude in mind, weigh the following scriptures against it:

205

Philippians 2:3-4

*3 Do nothing out of selfish ambition or vain
conceit. Rather, in humility value others above
yourselves,*

*4 not looking to your own interests but each of
you to the interests of the others.*

Does that line up with the interpretation of men with that
attitude? NO!

How about this one?

---

1 Corinthians 10:24

*No one should seek their own good, but the
good of others.*

So, then, what are verses 3-4 really saying?

---

*3 The husband should fulfill his marital duty to
his wife...*

Strong's Greek Lexicon

DUTY

Greek Word: Opheilé (of-i-lay')

Definition: a debt

From Help's Word-Studies

A specific (applied) kind of indebtedness, implying an "applied obligation" due to the debt (what is owed).

Specifically, of conjugal duty.

When you get a loan from a bank, they trust you will return the money back to them in full, along with the cost of getting the loan. What if you do not do that? We have problems! Your credit is damaged, the relationship with the bank is damaged, and it takes a while to restore your mess-up.

When you apply for a loan, whether it is with someone or an institution, they give you the "terms and conditions" of becoming a debtor to them. Then, you have the opportunity to agree or disagree with those terms and conditions. Most do not even read them and have no idea what they agreed to. Unfortunately, marriage is the same way.

When you said, "I do," you became a debtor to your wife, and she to you. Your responsibility as husband is to operate in that way even if your wife is not. It is called L-E-A-D-E-R-S-H-I-P! Jesus did the same thing without wavering!

Great news? This type of "debt" to the wife is a lot more fun to pay back than the debt to the bank! But for it to honor God, it must be done in the right context accompanied with the right heart condition. Selfishness never pleases God!

Romans 13:8

Let no debt remain outstanding, except the continuing debt to love one another, for whoever loves others has fulfilled the law.

So, the point is you are in debt to her. Approaching her with the command, "the Bible says you have to have sex with me!" does not work when you are the one in debt. That would be like telling the bank, "I owe you, so give me some money!"

To approach her in this way is of a selfish nature. The Bible instructs the wife to view you in the same way, but you do NOT use this as a weapon to get what you want. Always ask yourself the motive of your heart and decide if you are following God's heart, or yours.

---

4 The wife does not have authority over her own body but yields it to her husband. In the same way, the husband does not have authority over his own body but yields it to his wife.

Strong's Greek Lexicon

AUTHORITY

Greek Word: Exousiazó (ex-oo-see-ad'-zo)

Definition: To exercise authority over

Wait! That says, "I am to exercise authority over my wife's body!" Yes, but NO!

We can get a better understanding of this Greek word by exploring the root word.

Strong's Greek Lexicon

Greek Word: Exousia (ex-oo-see'-ah)

Definition: power to act, authority from

We can also find this same word for "authority" in the following verses. This will help get a better grasp of how this "authority" is used, and how you obtain it.

Luke 10:19

I have given you authority to trample on snakes and scorpions, and over all the power of the enemy. Nothing will harm you.

The key phrase: "I have given you authority."

---

1 Corinthians 9:12

If others have this right (exousia) of support from you, shouldn't we have it all the more? But we did not use this right (exousia). On the contrary, we put up with anything rather than hinder the gospel of Christ.

And…

Revelation 22:14

"Blessed are those who wash their robes, that they may have the right (exousia) to the tree of life and may go through the gates into the city.

Notice the theme? Put simply: "Delegated power."

Someone has to give you the authority or, "power to act" over something.

In Luke 10:19, the authority Jesus gives us is based on our faith. As strong as your faith will determine how strong your authority is. Maybe, just maybe… how selfless you are as a husband just may get you more authority from your wife. If it does not, you still must walk in selflessness.

---

4 The wife does not have authority over her own body but yields it to her husband…

When your wife "yields" her body to you, you must be a good steward over her body much like we are to be good stewards of our money. Your role as husband is to "take care of your wife!" If you are selfish in your approach and only thinking of you and what YOU can get out of it, you are NOT being a Godly Strong husband!

Your very first priority in the bedroom is, shockingly enough, your wife! What a beautiful moment when the wife gives you authority over her body, allowing you to do whatever you want (that you both agree to) in order to take care of her. That sounds more like what God would want during sex than the faulty interpretation mentioned at the beginning.

This is also an exciting time to "submit one to another out of reverence for Christ!" You are honoring your wife by putting her first, which means you are in obedience to God which is a form of worship, and not being selfish is certainly being "under God's arrangement (hupotassó)."

Now, let's revisit the verses above to learn if they line up with this way of thinking; where you put your wife as priority so that when you have power to act over her body, she is well pleased and fulfilled because you are not thinking of yourself, but her.

Shall we say, "satisfying" a debt?

Philippians 2:3-4

3 Do nothing out of selfish ambition or vain conceit. Rather, in humility value others above yourselves,

4 not looking to your own interests but each of you to the interests of the others.

Yes sir! Lines up beautifully!

1 Corinthians 10:24

24 No one should seek their own good, but the good of others.

P-E-R-F-E-C-T!

There is a parallel here from when you got married. When your wife said, "I do," what she was really saying was, "I am entrusting my life to you, to take care of me and do what is best for me and our family."

When she "yields her body to you," it is the same principle. She is trusting you to do what is best for her, taking care of her like a real man is supposed to; putting her F-I-R-S-T!

Sacrificial love, selflessness, servanthood… all characteristics of Jesus. We are not to lose sight of these things, even in the bedroom.

Finally, we will examine two parts of verse 5 (5A and 5B).

To preface verse 5, when we owe someone and do not pay it, that would technically make us a thief! We just stole from whom we owe the debt.

211

5A Do not deprive each other except perhaps by mutual consent and for a time, so that you may devote yourselves to prayer.

Strong's Greek Lexicon

DEPRIVE

Greek Word: Aposteró (ap-os-ter-eh'-o)

Definition: to defraud, deprive of

Aposteréō comes from the two words:

Greek Word:	Apó	Stereóō
Definition:	Away from	Deprive

Properly: Keep away from someone, i.e., by defrauding (depriving); to cheat, taking away what rightfully belongs to someone else.

Simply put: To ROB! Yep, that would make you a thief if you were unwilling to be sexually intimate with her.

There is even a spiritual element to this where you can use sex as a weapon! How so?

5B Then come together again so that Satan will not tempt you because of your lack of self-control.

When your wife is satisfied, the likelihood of her mind wandering is much less. We also understand that in our fallen nature, some will still walk in the flesh. Regardless of that exception, having sex

– and lots of it – is just another way we can defeat the enemy and his evil schemes. Cool, huh?

The only time this scripture says to NOT have sex is during prayer. When you are not in a time of prayer, it says to "come together." The conclusion is that there is only one-time sexual unity should not be occurring.

Sex is good and created by God. We are to manage it carefully as He has given us the responsibility to be "wise stewards of the wife's body."

The Godly Strong Rhema Translation

---

1 Corinthians 7:3-5

3 The husband should fulfill his marital debt to his wife, and likewise the wife to her husband.

4 The wife should give her husband the power to act over her body just as the husband gives his wife power to act over his with the goal of pleasing the other.

5 Do not rob each other except perhaps by mutual consent and for a time, so that you may devote yourselves to prayer.

Then get back to having sex so that Satan will not tempt you because of your lack of self-control; defeating the enemy all while having fun doing it!

If, IF we would all – husbands and wives - respond toward each other in this way, the bedroom would be hot, steamy, and dynamic!

What? Your wife has not caught on yet? Another great moment to lead her by example!

Lastly, regarding this scripture:

It is perfectly ok, and even strongly encouraged, to share with your wife your likes, your dislikes, your desires, etc. Why? Because this scripture tells her to be a good steward of your body, too! She needs to know what you enjoy in the bedroom in order to make it happen, right? Right! Just make sure you do not put your needs above hers and operate unselfishly. Communicate, talk about it, learn what you each are comfortable with, and let the fun begin!

Look how steamy it is when two people act with mutual consent.

Song of Songs 5:16

His mouth is sweetness itself; he is altogether lovely. This is my beloved, this is my friend,

---

How would she know his mouth is sweetness? She would have to taste it, right?

One more Hebrew word for the road...

Strong's Hebrew Lexicon

SWEETNESS

Hebrew Word: Mamthaqqim (mam-tak')

Definition: Sweetness, sweet things

In this context according to Brown-Driver-Briggs ?

"A lover's kisses!"

But one thing you must not miss in this particular scripture:

"This is my beloved (another word for LOVER), this is my friend."

Both – lover and friend - are what he is to her. Are you that to your wife?

Song of Songs 4:16

Awake, north wind, and come, south wind! Blow on my garden, that its fragrance may spread everywhere. Let my beloved come into his garden and taste its choice fruits.

Symbolism, anybody?

Song of Songs 7:7-8

7 Your stature is like that of the palm, and your breasts like clusters of fruit.

8 I said, "I will climb the palm tree; I will take hold of its fruit."

You translate those on your own.

The Godly Strong Challenge

Sit down and read the last two devotionals with your wife to get on the same page about God's design for sex. Discuss together in what ways you may not be operating within God's guidelines.

After you review these things with your wife, both of you go practice on getting to know each other better than ever.... like, NOW!

The Godly Strong Challenge #2:

Read the entire book of Song of Songs. Notice the compliments they share with each other. The pure admiration they have (timios) and notice how many of those compliments are above the neck!

The Godly Strong Challenge #3

She is not to only be your lover, but your friend. So, if that part is missing (friend), make sure you rekindle that with her because, in case you missed it, emotional intimacy comes before sexual intimacy. And all of it is to glorify God!

PUT YOUR BEST FOOT FORWARD

The Grand Finale!

For this exercise you will need to have:

- Humility
- Sacrificial love
- Humbleness
- The attitude of a bond servant
- Boldness
- Compassion
- A giving of yourself
- A selfless attitude
- A servant's mindset
- Agape Love

If you want out of this, you will need:

- Arrogance
- Pride
- Selfishness
- A "me first" attitude
- Conditional love
- Hardness of heart
- Weakness
- Thinking more highly of yourself than you should
- Stubbornness

As the husband, you are about to do exactly what Jesus did (if you have the necessary components in list #1)! Just like Jesus, it takes a Godly Strong husband to pull this off with the attitude God desires. Make a point RIGHT NOW to have a mindset of pushing through with determination and a "no excuses" attitude. Jesus said if you do this, you will be blessed! Along with that blessing, you will have accomplished one of the most beautiful acts in history. Oh yeah, there is a REALLY good chance your wife will be immensely blessed, too!

This action fits all of Genesis 2:24:

- Spiritual Intimacy
- Emotional Intimacy
- Physical Intimacy

Ready? Here we go! Read and be determined! You've got this!

John 13:6-8

6 (Jesus) came to Simon Peter, who said to him, "Lord, are you going to wash my feet?"

7 Jesus replied, "You do not realize now what I am doing, but later you will understand."

8 "No," said Peter, "you shall never wash my feet."

Jesus answered, "Unless I wash you, you have no part with me."

Watch what is next, after Jesus led by example:

John 13:14-15, 17

14 Now that I, your Lord and Teacher, have washed your feet, you also should wash one another's feet.

15 I have set you an example that you should do as I have done for you.

17 Now that you know these things, you will be blessed if you do them.

Wait, you still do not want to wash the feet of your wife? Maybe you should keep in mind that Jesus even washed the feet of Judas, who was about to betray Him, and Jesus knew that!

There is something "spiritual" about this beautiful act of worship toward God when you humble yourself for this purpose.

Not only did Jesus wash the feet of Judas, he removed His outer wear, wrapped a towel around His waist, and dried their feet with it; imitating how a true servant would do it.

This takes an enormous amount of humility and humbleness. It might not seem like the most glamourous thing to do, but that is not the point of what is truly an act of worship.

There is something supernatural about this act that is out of this world! And if you and your wife are on a bit of rocky ground, this very well may start the healing process and reconnect the both of you.

"Are you crazy?! I am not doing that!"

Whose example are you following, then? Sounds like list #2 fits you more accurately if this is your attitude.

The Godly Strong Challenge

Put on your favorite love song like the one you first danced to (as long as it's not vulgar!), play some praise music (whatever clean music that sets the tone), dim the lights, get some candles, get her some flowers, and as you wash her feet, let her know how much you love her, appreciate her, and how thankful you are to be her husband. It is going to be an emotional – but beautiful – moment for you both!

Now, get a bowl of water, a wash rag, and tick off Satan while worshipping God and honoring your wife! Wash her feet and love her like THE MAN!

CHALLENGE QUESTIONS

How did your wife react?

How did it make you feel?

Document here what you and your wife experienced in this beautiful moment:

HINT: You can do it more than once as the years go by, even if it just "because!"

A MODEL WORTH IMITATING

To conclude, we will head back to the beginning of the scriptures. Why? This is where we find the marriage model implemented by God Himself. It is the foundation on which our marriage should be built and implements the necessary intimacies for a healthy marriage.

Genesis 2:24

"(A) For this reason, (B) a man shall leave his father and his mother and (C) be joined to his wife; and (D) they shall become one flesh."

Following is a chart to help you observe more clearly what has been presented throughout this book.

The Marriage Model

	Literal	*Figurative*	*Intimacy Type*
A	*By God's design*	*By God's design*	*Spiritual*
B	*Abandon parents*	*Leave past behind*	*Spiritual*
C	*Hold tight (like glue)*	*Hotly pursue wife*	*Emotional*
D	*Have sex*	*P.U.T.*	*Physical/Sexual*

But wait! There's more!

Watch how marriage - as we know it - correlates to us being the "Bride of Christ."

SPIRITUAL INTIMACY

- By God's design a man shall leave his old life behind...

---

2 Corinthians 5:17

Therefore, if anyone is in Christ, the new creation has come: The old has gone, the new is here!

EMOTIONAL INTIMACY

- Learning to "hotly pursue" someone other than yourself...

Proverbs 8:17

I love those who love me, and those who diligently seek me will find me.

PHYSICAL/SEXUAL INTIMACY

- The two become one body...

- *1 Corinthians 12:27*

- *Now you are the body of Christ, and each one of you is a part of it.*

Operating in your marriage by God's design is powerful! It will not only bless you and your wife and help you grow, but it will have a major impact on those around you whether they admit it or not.

The Three Intimacies

SPIRITUAL INTIMACY

This type of intimacy requires being in tune with God. It requires pursuit and an intimate connection of "knowing" Him. This is the #1 priority to have a marriage God has called you to have. It is difficult to operate the way God wants you to in marriage if you do not recognize His voice. Without this intimacy, your marriage will never reach the purpose God has for it. It all starts by leaving your past behind.

EMOTIONAL INTIMACY

#2 in the intimacy department is emotional. When we date, we pursue. "How you got them is how you keep them." But many stop the pursuit once marriage happens. This is backwards, according to scripture.

Pursuing your wife creates emotional intimacy with her, and that is to NEVER cease, much like our pursuit of God!

PHYSICAL/SEXUAL INTIMACY

Just because the head of the wife is the husband, that does not make the husband more important than the wife. There just has to be an order. In the same way, just because sexual intimacy is 3rd in the "law of order" does not mean it is any less important. But God wants the gift of sex to be a gift to us in our marriage, and His design is for there to be an emotional connection to make the sexual activity is more fulfilling when we become "one body" with her.

CONCLUSION

Being a Christian means that we "leave our past behind," "pursue God," and become "one body" with Him.

Being a Godly Strong husband means that we "leave our past behind," "hotly pursue the wife," and become "one body" with her.

That, my friend, is the marriage model!

Now we can see clearly what it means when Paul wrote:

Ephesians 5:32

This is a profound mystery—but I am talking about Christ and the church.

CHALLENGE QUESTIONS

What would an unbeliever think about Christ if the only thing they knew about Him was the example of your marriage?

What would an unbeliever think of Christ if the only example they had was the way you treat your wife?

Your Godly Strong overview

The Godly Strong Challenge

It is time, if you have not already, to recognize and implement the four basic components of marriage listed above that are created by God.

For a healthy marriage, ensure they are being developed on a continual basis.

The way you treat your bride is an indication to the world of how Christ treats His bride. Your goal and challenge from here on out are to display the best example you are able to fulfill that marital purpose so that...

He may receive the glory!

CONTACT and INFO

Information:

John Helton, "The Blind Fury" is the founder / President of The Blood Wall Ministries, Inc., a 501C3.

Our Ministries

- Marital Monkey (www.MaritalMonkey.com)
- Godly Strong for Husbands (A division of Marital Monkey)
- The Blind Fury Speaking Ministries (www.TheBlindFury.com)

Services:

- Marriage coaching and mentoring
- Husband coaching and mentoring
- Self-Development Coaching
- Premarital Counseling
- Free online and interactive workshops
- Christian inspirational speaking including:
    - General speaking engagements
    - Men's Conferences
    - Marriage Conferences

CONTACT

The Blood Wall Ministries, Inc.

- Contact@TheBlindFury.com
- Www.TheBlindFury.com
- Www.MaritalMonkey.com

The ministries of The Blood Wall are primarily donation based; therefore, we would love for you to consider becoming a monthly partner to help us see marriages transformed, husbands to step it up in a Godly Strong way, and continue with the current and future ministries of The Blood Wall!

Please visit the Marital Monkey website to become a monthly partner!

Other books:

STOP YOUR WHINING: Legally Blind with 20/20 Vision

the inspirational story of John's response to losing vision as well as becoming a widower. It is sure to encourage you, challenge you, and even make you laugh.

Pick it up on Amazon or at John's website for a donation.

Made in the USA
Monee, IL
29 May 2023